Go Tell The World

By Jimmy Maynor

International Standard Book Number: 0-89350-002-X
3rd Printing

Published by Jimmy Maynor Ministries
P. O. Box 2428
Cleveland, Tennessee 37311

Cover Art Work done by Earl M. Reed

Printed in United States of America

FOREWORD

My name is Norvel Hayes. I would like to introduce you to a man I have known nearly all of my life. I take great pleasure in introducing this book to America. I know that it will be a great blessing to everyone who reads it. It is the miracle-working power of God in action. I believe this book has the power to change your complete life. Jimmy Maynor is the key person in the story you are about to read in the first part of this book.

I went to school with Jimmy and I know that the story is true as to what God has done for him. I know that at the age of twelve, Jimmy just stopped growing and no one knew the reason why. His parents could not figure out what had happened to their child. At the age of 18, when Jimmy went to take a physical for the army, the record showed that he was four feet and nine and one-half inches tall, and weighed ninety-three pounds.

Jimmy has always had a call on his life to work for God. He was always a good-natured boy. God wanted Jimmy to work for Him, but he refused. God tried to be merciful to Jimmy like he does to everyone. Because of rebellion, Jimmy had a car wreck one night. He was in a hospital dying but God showed mercy through the prayer of concerned Christians, and spared his life. There were long weeks and months that Jimmy stayed in bed, and in a wheelchair, going back and forth to the doctor in an ambulance which grew very tiresome.

So, one day Jimmy decided he would get into the Bible and see what God said. He was fearful and depressed, afraid that he would never walk again, but by reading the Bible, he found out that God did not give him the spirit of fear; but of power, and love, and a sound mind. He then began to put his trust in God and prayed that God would heal him. In three weeks, the X-rays showed that he was healed. His body began to grow and in one year, he was six feet one inch tall and weighed 175 pounds. This just shows the great miracle-working power of God. He gave his life completely to God and began witnessing to people about the saving power of God and the miracle-working power of God.

He became a witnessing teacher and began to teach soul-winning classes in many churches. He teaches how to train teams of people to witness from house to house, and win the lost for Christ.

In 1973, Jimmy began to travel with me in my teaching ministry. He taught witnessing in the morning, and I would teach at night. Sometimes he also taught on healing and God's miracle-working power. In the afternoon he would take people out from house to house and train them how to witness effectively. People who sat under his ministry and witnessed with him from house to house received a change in their lives.

His witnessing ministry is the best I have ever seen, and I know that your heart is going to be stirred, and your heart is going to be thrilled from the top of your head to the bottom of your feet when you read this book. It is amazing what God can do through a man like Jimmy who is yielded to do the will of God. I suggest that you read this book and pass it on to your friends so they too, can hear this story of the MIRACLE-WORKING POWER OF GOD.

Norvel Hayes

CONTENTS

PREFACE

For the past few years I have directed soul-winning seminars in various churches. Statistics show that a very, very small percentage of all Christians ever lead a soul to Christ. In many churches today, we have wonderful healing services, miracle services, etc., but not much is said about soul-winning.

Jesus said that His meat was "to do the will of the Father" (John 4:34). And in Matthew 18:14 we read: "Even so it is not the will of your Father which is in heaven, that one of these little ones should perish." Jesus gave His life so His Father's will could be done. What are we doing about it?

When a man leaves a will, it contains directions as to the distribution of his property after his death. Jesus also left a "will" for His followers: "Go ye therefore, and teach all nations, baptizing them in the name of the Father, and of the Son, and of the Holy Ghost: Teaching them to observe all things whatsoever I have commanded you: and lo, I am with you alway, even unto the end of the world" (Matt. 28:19-20).

This is the will of God for us! When I first started witnessing, I had no plan. I didn't know what to say. I was filled with fear. As I travel across the country, I find countless others who feel the same way.

This book is written to these Christians who are struggling with the conviction that they should speak out for Jesus. They should witness when they have an opportunity, but they just never do. It contains my testimony of how the Lord touched my life, and how from a very humble beginning of witnessing, I have had the privilege of introducing thousands of people to Jesus Christ.

I trust and pray that this book will be a help to you, and that you will do your part in carrying out the will of God.

Jimmy Maynor

ACKNOWLEDGMENT

Special thanks and much appreciation to Mrs. Elmer Saylor for her typing and editing assistance.

"Sticks and Stones"

"Sticks and stones can hurt my bones, but names can never hurt me." I know we have all heard this saying lots of times, but it is far from the truth. How many times I found this so during my childhood and teen-age years.

I had quit growing when I was twelve years old. At 18 when I took an army physical, their records show that I was four feet, nine and one-half inches tall and weighed ninety-three pounds. I was a small person, alone in a real big, cold, cruel world. I was lonely, depressed, and defeated. It seemed like no one in the world loved me or cared for me except my family. In school, I was always the smallest boy, and most of the girls were bigger than I was, too. I was an outcast. People called me names that were cruel, and which I hated and despised. They would call me PEE-WEE, RUNT, and some others that I dare not print. Names can hurt *MORE* than sticks and stones. I longed to hear people call me by my real name, but very few ever did.

In grammar school I was kicked around like a football. I was scared to go to school because I knew that some bigger boy would be picking on me or twisting my arm, or just hurting me because I was different. Children can be very cruel to those who are different.

9

When I got to high school, I was not hurt as bad, but I was, of course, the smallest person there, and I was still made fun of and called bad names. I was always the blunt of a joke. People loved to play tricks on me. They thought it was funny and laughed, but inside I would be crying.

I finished high school and took a physical for the army. Even they did not want me. I was too small. I wanted to go to college. I knew that as small as I was, I would need to train in some field for a decent job. Again I was defeated because my parents were farmers, and they could not afford to send me to college. At this time there were no government loans to help people to go to college.

So I began seeking employment. I would go to the same places my friends did, but no one would give me a job. They would tell me that I was too small to do the work. One man laughed and said, "Come back when you grow up." To him it was a joke, but, believe me, it was no joke to me! The world out there was a big old mean world to me. I tried to get other jobs, but failed. Finally, in desperation, I began to apply for jobs in grocery stores just carrying out groceries as a bag boy. I had done well in school, but I ended up carrying out groceries for $2 per day. This was not during the lean depression years, either. This was in the 1950's. My friends were making $12 per day.

Later, I landed a job working in a drug store as a fountain boy, making $3 per day. I worked twelve hours a day and worked at this job four years, until I was 22 years old. At that time I did not even have a car that I could drive. I was so small I could not drive my Dad's pick-up truck. I wanted to date some girls, but did not have any transportation.

Those were lonely, desperate years. Sometimes my so-called friends would get me a blind date with a girl. This was done just for a joke, because she would always be about a foot taller than I was. They would get a big laugh out of this, but it was not funny to me. My life was a life of confusion. I was a very lonely person, but I managed to cover it up and put on a good act. I didn't want anyone to know that the names were hurting much more than sticks or stones ever could.

THE ACCIDENT

I was saved at the age of sixteen, and went to church every time the doors were open. But I was just a nominal Christain, living a defeated life. I was cold and indifferent. I thought that God had dealt me an unfair blow. I couldn't understand why I had to be so small.

When I was twenty-three years old, God began to deal with me about working for Him and cleaning up my life. The young people in church looked on me as one of them, but not as an adult. They loved me and wanted me to work with them. But I told them I did not have time. I was too busy just doing my own thing. (When we are doing our own thing, we are really doing the devil's thing.) I was not interested in working with a bunch of kids. I was mad at God and the whole world for the way I had been treated. I felt I had been dealt a terrible blow by having to go through life as I had. Everything I ever wanted out of life was just beyond my reach.

Several years passed, and I had not done anything for Jesus. I was stubborn and rebellious. God began to convict me of my sins and tried to get me to come to Him and give my life to Him 100 percent. I was attending church because I had been taught it was the right thing to do. But I was not interested in spiritual things. I was living my life the way I wanted to live it. Not that I was in deep sin, because God's power was on my life so much that if I drank

11

or gambled, He would convict me so much that I could not sleep at night. I was a very miserable person running from God.

God says that He chastens those He loves, and if He chastens them not, they are none of His. In Revelation 3:19 it says, "AS MANY AS I LOVE, I REBUKE AND CHASTEN: BE ZEALOUS THEREFORE AND RE-PENT." I did not repent, and this is what happened to me:

One night I was riding in a car with a friend when a car hit us head-on doing around 90 miles an hour. My knee hit the dash of the car and drove the knee bone into my hip, breaking it in three places. They picked me up in an ambulance and took me to a local hospital. They just shook their heads and sent me on to a larger hospital in Chattanooga, Tennessee.

When they examined me, they found that six pints of my blood had just disappeared. My temperature was sky-high, and my blood pressure was very bad. Nearly every gland in my body was malfunctioning. The doctor told my Dad that I was one of the most severe shock cases he had ever seen, and that he didn't think I would survive.

Sometime in the morning before daylight, I became conscious. I realized I was dying and that I was not in a right relationship with God. I knew that out there some-where people were praying for me. I could feel wave after wave of love sweeping over me.

Then I began talking to God. I said, "God, I have never done one thing for you. I have never told one per-son about you, Lord. If you will forgive me of my sins and let me live, I will work for you."

I repented of my sins. I prayed a prayer of confes-sion, and I felt the weight of sin lift from me. I knew that He had forgiven me, and that He cared very much for me.

"If we confess our sins, He is faithful and just to forgive us our sins, and to cleanse us from all unrighteousness" (I John 1:9).

The doctor did not think that I would live, but by daylight I was coming out of the critical stage. Thank God, for Doctor Jesus. Five doctors at Mayo Clinic may say you have to die, but what does Doctor Jesus say? "HIMSELF TOOK OUR INFIRMITIES, AND BARE OUR SICKNESSES." One touch from Jesus is all anyone needs.

Seven days later, I was operated on. The splintered bone was taken out, and they put in four stainless-steel bolts, five inches long, in my hip to hold it together. They also used stainless-steel wire to hold my bones together. The doctor did not believe that I would ever walk again on that leg. After six weeks in the hospital, my bones were still not healing at all, but they said I could go home if I would be careful, and stay in bed. I could be up a little while each day in the wheelchair with someone helping me so as not to put any weight on the broken leg.

Each month the ambulance would come and take me to Chattanooga for X-rays, but each time the doctor would shake his head and say my bones were not healing. They put me on a special diet to see if that would help, but it didn't. I had been in bed over eight months by this time, and I was very fearful that I would never walk again. Little did I know what the Lord had in store for me.

13
A NEW MAN

During the seven months I was bedridden after the accident, I read comic books, fiction books, Westerns, sports magazines, all kinds of literature, and watched T.V. Everything, except read the Bible. Matthew 22:29 says, "Ye do err, not knowing the scriptures, nor the power of

God." How the devil loves to keep us away from God's Word so that we will be weak and ignorant of His will and His power. He'll put all kinds of things in front of us to keep our attention away from the Word, because he knows the Word is truth, and the truth will set us free from the enemy.

One day, however, I opened the Word as I lay in bed. I thought perhaps I could find an answer there. Before opening the Bible, I prayed God to show me what I needed to know. I just let the Bible fall open, and a Scripture just seemed to jump out at me: "For God hath not given us the spirit of fear; but of power, and of love, and of a sound mind" (II Tim. 1:7). I saw that the fear that I had was not of God, but of Satan, and I saw that fear was a spirit.

I opened the Bible again, and it fell open to I John 4:18, "Perfect love casteth out fear; because fear hath torment. He that feareth is not made perfect in love." I realized that if I had faith in God, if I had trust in God, if I totally gave myself to Him, I didn't have to worry about anything. If I believed His Word, then I could have faith in Him and trust Him, and I would never have to be fearful anymore. He loved me and cared for me, and I needed to cast all my cares upon Him (I Pet. 5:7).

The third time, the Bible fell open to James 4:7-8, "Submit yourselves therefore to God. Resist the devil, and he will flee from you. Draw nigh to God, and he will draw nigh to you." In this scripture I saw two things:

1. Submit yourself to God.
2. Resist the devil and he will flee.

I had already given my life to God, but I had not yet resisted the devil. I had obeyed Step one, and I was now ready to obey Step two. I said, "Devil, I come against you in the Name of Jesus, the King of kings, and the Lord of lords, and I resist this fear and depression you have been troubling me with, and I command all fear and depression to go from me now."

Praise God! I felt the spirit of fear and the depressing spirits go, and the peace of God began to saturate me from the top of my head to the tip of my toes. His love moved over me, wave after wave after wave. Words cannot describe how I felt. I felt the peace that passeth all understanding. Before this time, I had lain awake at night and was so depressed and fearful that I would cry. But after this experience, I was never fearful or depressed again because when I obeyed His Word, the love of Jesus set me free.

I was so excited about the Bible. I began to read it and found out what it said about healing. I had been told that healing was not for today, that miracles were not for today, etc. I had been told this went out with the Apostles.

I saw where the Bible said to lay hands on the sick, and they would recover. But no one in my church ever did that, so I could not call for anyone to lay hands on me. I began to take God's Word for what it said. It said that He wanted to heal His children.

I discovered there are some conditions to healing. One of these is *faith*. I found what faith is: "Now faith is the substance of things hoped for, the evidence of things not seen" (Heb. 11:1). In other words, you have to believe that you have it before you get it, and then you will get it.

I saw in Mark 11:24 that it said, "What things soever ye desire, when ye pray, believe that ye receive them, and ye shall have them." It had been over eight months since the accident, and my bones had not healed. In my church they preached mostly salvation, and this is the best part. To be born of the spirit is the most important thing, but if you already are saved, you need to know something else. I was sick, and I needed to know about healing. I had never had

15

one person tell me anything about how to be healed. All they knew to do was to depend on the doctor. The doctors do all they can. The doctors had done all they could for me, but they could in no way make my bones heal. But God says in His Word that if we will pray the prayer of faith, we will be healed. Not every time instantly, but when we stand in faith and don't waver or doubt, we will receive in due time.

One day as I was lying in bed, I prayed and said, "Lord, I ask you to heal me according to your Word. I base my faith on Mark 11:24. I believe that I receive my healing, and I thank you now, for I believe I am healed."

I wanted to confess my healing, and I called my mother and said, "Mother, don't worry any more about me, for I am going to be all right. I prayed and asked Jesus to heal me."

I knew that she had been worrying about me, as mother's will. She asked me, "Jimmy, son, do you feel any better?"

I told her I did not. I could see this was troubling her. On one hand, I said I was healed and was going to be all right. On the other hand, I said I was not feeling any better. But I was in the spirit, and she was in the natural. Faith says, "I am healed, even if I don't feel any better."

Bless her heart! She just did not understand the principle of faith. Faith says, "I am not going on *feeling,* but on *faith.* I have it now by *faith.*"

I began to confess that I was healed. To be saved, you must believe in your heart and confess with your mouth that Jesus is Lord. I figured that if it would work for salvation it would work for healing. Too many people are living by feelings, and they cannot receive the things of God. We are living in two worlds—the natural and the supernatural. We must come out of the natural and into the supernatural to receive things from God. The natural senses say you are

16

not healed, but faith says you are.

Three weeks after I had prayed and confessed I was healed. The ambulance came to take me to Chattanooga for X-rays again. I *knew* that the X-rays would show I was healed. You might ask me how I knew. I cannot tell you that. I just knew that I knew that I knew, and there was absolutely no doubt. After taking the X-rays, the doctor said, "This is impossible. Bones don't heal in four weeks."

But, praise God, mine had, because I had gotten in touch with the great Physician, and His name is Jesus! *Praise God forevermore!*

It wasn't long until I was up and about my Father's business. I began to work with the young people at our church. I was on fire for God. I could not do enough for Him as He had done so much for me. At the time of my healing, I was just concerned about getting well. I had not thought about asking God to let my body grow. Of course, my heart's desire through the years was to be normal like other people. And in the past, I had prayed many prayers to be normal. My prayers were not answered because I was a sinner, rebelling against God, and I was not praying in faith. But all of a sudden one day, I happened to notice that my pants legs were a little too short. It wasn't long until they were even shorter. PRAISE GOD! Jesus began to make my body grow. And I *grew* and *grew* until one year later, when I was 27 years old, I was 6 feet, one-inch tall, and weighed 175 pounds.

You just don't grow when you are 26 years old, but I did! Jesus loves me, and He can do anything! And HE DID IT FOR ME! "If any man be in Christ, he is a new creature" (II Cor. 5:17) has a double meaning for me.

Now I travel all over the country praying for the sick and see many miracles of legs and arms that are too short that are lengthened by the power of God. . . . .some three or four inches. *WHO KNOWS, SOME DAY THE LORD MAY LET ME PRAY FOR SHORT PEOPLE TO GROW TALLER BY THE POWER OF GOD!*

Without a Vision, the People Perish

"And daily in the temple, and in every house, they ceased not to teach and preach Jesus Christ" (Acts 5:42).

The Church of Jesus Christ is in a new time and place in history. In times past, we have had great revivals. Men like Charles Finney and D. L. Moody and early dynamic evangelists won thousands of souls to Christ. Even now we have a few men like Billy Graham who hold huge crusades, leading many people to Jesus. But as time goes on, it is getting harder and harder to get the lost people to go hear the Gospel preached in the churches.

Churches have an idea that if they can only get the sinners to church, they will be saved. So what do they do? They build large impressive buildings, some costing millions of dollars. They put in the best carpets, and they have air-conditioning, with nice padded pews so the people can be comfortable. They have magnificent organs and many musical instruments. And some even have orchestras. Then they bring in a special speaker with much advertising, asking the people to come and hear their speaker. They advertise by television, newspaper, radio, and have special singers, quartets, and choirs.

What happens? The faithful church members come, and this is good. But what about the lost people? Why

19

didn't they come? We invited them. Why didn't they come? The church desires to win souls to Christ Jesus and works hard to get them to come to their church. They have everything ready for them when they get there. They pray for them to come and are sure if they come, they will be saved. They have a fine pastor, one of the best in the country. They have a fine staff of personal workers ready for action; ready to bring the ones who come to acknowledge Jesus as their personal Saviour. But *why* won't they come? Why, with all the efforts they have put forth, won't they come to church and give their life to Christ?

The idea seemed to be a good one. It was good for the few who did come and were saved. The reason more did not come is simple. SINNERS DO NOT GO TO CHURCH, and the church is failing, failing, failing, because 90 percent of the lost just will not go to church.

What is the answer? We find it in the Word of God. "And daily in the temple, and in every house, they ceased not to teach and preach Jesus Christ" (Acts 5:42). Acts 2:47 reads, "And the Lord added to the church daily such as should be saved." The Lord will only add daily if we witness daily. Did only the ordained ministers teach and preach daily? No! No! No! Each memeber witnessed! Laymen witnessed!

Thousands were being saved, because the whole body of Christ was witnessing. They were going out door-to-door, house-to-house—telling the good news of the Lord Jesus Christ. They went out, and people were added to the church daily. Acts 6:7 tells us, "And the word of God increased; and the number of the disciples multiplied in Jerusalem greatly." The early church was getting results. In Acts 19:10 there is a startling fact: "And this continued by the space of two years; so that all they which dwelt in Asia heard the word of the Lord Jesus, both Jews and Greeks."

In the short space of only two years, it says ALL who dwelled in Asia heard the word. What have we done in two years? If the early church had done like today's church is doing, just going to church Sunday morning and Sunday night, and Wednesday night, they would have failed to get the word out to the lost and dying world, just as we are failing in our day to get the word out to a lost and dying world.

"Where there is no vision, the people perish" (Prov. 29:18). There are millions of lost men, women, boys, and girls going to hell because Christians have no vision. We need to be about our Father's business. We need to return to being like the early church was, which is the only way to reach the world for Christ. True, the big crusades have their part, but only a small part. In the early church, they went where the people were, and they began to tell them what Jesus had done. The greatest witness you will ever give is to tell people what Jesus means to you. This is something that you have experienced, and something that you can tell.

The early church people also shared the Word of God. Unless we share the Word with people, they are not going to be saved. We must share the Word of God! Too many times we go out and invite people to come to church and even tell them how wonderful Jesus is, but we don't tell them words whereby they can be saved. A lost person cannot be saved unless someone goes to him and tells him *how*. "How then shall they call on him in whom they have not believed? and how shall they believe in him of whom they have not heard? and how shall they hear without a preacher? And how shall they preach, except they be sent? as it is written, how beautiful are the feet of them that preach the gospel of peace, and bring glad tidings of good things! But they have not all obeyed the gospel. For Esaias saith, Lord, who hath believed our report? So then faith

21

cometh by hearing, and hearing by the word of God" (Rom. 10:14-17).

You can go to Christian retreat camps, seminars, shepherd's retreats, etc., and they can teach you on faith, healing, deliverance, and many other subjects, and these are all very needful. But we have a great need of being taught on witnessing, too. It's true that this is not a desirable subject. I can teach on healing, and we'll have a full house. But when I teach witnessing, not many people show up. Most of us fail when it comes to witnessing, and we don't want to be reminded of this. The leaders of our youth camps and other camps and retreats need to teach witnessing. It is the *number one* thing needed today. Winning souls is more important than anything else. The most important thing that ever happened is when I was saved. It wasn't when you were healed. It wasn't when you were baptized in the Holy Spirit, as important as these things are.

"For the Son of man is come to save that which was lost. How think ye? If a man have an hundred sheep, and one of them be gone astray, doth he not leave the ninety and nine, and goeth into the mountains, and seeketh that which is gone astray? And if so be that he find it, verily I say unto you, he rejoiceth more of that sheep, than of the ninety and nine which went not astray. Even so it is not the will of your Father which is in heaven, that one of these little ones should perish" (Matt. 18:11-14).

The purpose of Jesus' coming into the world was to seek and save the lost. In His High Priestly prayer, Jesus said: "As thou has sent me into the world, even so have I also sent them into the world" (John 17:18). Our purpose, then, in the world is also to seek and save the lost. Notice, it says to *SEEK* the lost. To seek someone, you go looking for them. You do not expect them to come to you.

For years, people thought only the clergy or pastor's

were to preach. The word "preach" as it is found in the Bible, refers more to witnessing than it does to preaching in a church. In Lester Sumrall's book, *Fishers of Men,* he tells us the word preach occurs 112 times in the New Testament—106 times, he says, it is used in relation to a personal witness for Christ, rather than a minister preaching in a church. "Ye are my witnesses." Witness is the key word in the New Testament. It occurs 175 times. Every disciple of Christ is a witness. A witness is under obligation to tell what he knows.

Who are the preachers then? They are you and I, and every Christian. And what is successful witnessing? I like to use the definition given by Bill Bright of Campus Crusade: "Successful witnessing is simply sharing Christ in the power of the Holy Spirit and leaving the results to God." We are not going out witnessing under our own power, for we would truly fail. We are going in the power of the King of kings and Lord of lords. He will add such as should be saved.

I have been teaching witnessing for years and have had many pastors tell me that they have been pastoring a church themselves for years and do not know how to witness outside the church building. We have gone out many times teaching witnessing and soul-winning, and I have asked the pastor if he would like to go with me witnessing, and he would say, "Jimmy, if you don't care, would you just lead. I haven't had much experience in witnessing door-to-door."

In a city near me, a pastor caught a vision of getting his members trained in soul-winning. They had a witnessing seminar, but only a few came. Those who came were mostly young people, but they received training on how to witness. The young people caught a vision of people going to hell and began to witness once a week on Saturdays. In one month, thirty people were won to Christ—more than

23

the church had won in a year.

Most churches are not winning souls. Last year I had a training seminar on personal soul-winning in a church that was a Full Gospel Church. They had wonderful singing and a wonderful praise time. They had been doing a wonderful job in teaching faith, healing, deliverance, etc. The presence of Jesus was felt, and from all outward appearances, you would say this was a very successful church. But they were not winning very many souls. They were missing the mark.

We can go to church and enjoy what God is doing and how He is moving upon His people doing great and marvelous things. And God wants us to enjoy His blessings, but He wants us to be a blessing to others. He wants us to tell people with whom we come in contact each week about Him. Most of all, people need to get saved. They are doomed to hell unless we catch the vision the early church had and begin to spread the Good News that Jesus cares, and that Jesus saves. He will save anyone who comes to Him, but how can they come unless the church goes and tells them words whereby they can be saved?

How Jesus
Taught Me to Witness

After God healed me, I was so grateful to Him. I wanted to be a soul-winner to show my gratitude. I began to go out with the church on visitation nights, but I wasn't very successful because I was so fearful. I had never been taught to witness. I would go to people's homes and knock on the door, hoping they wouldn't be home, because I was so scared.

I wanted to witness, and I had a desire to witness, but I didn't have the boldness that I needed. I wanted to witness well, because I loved Jesus so much because of what He had done for me. I had learned when I got healed that God has not given us the spirit of fear, but power, and love, and a sound mind. So I overcame this obstacle. I got bolder, and I began to witness more.

As I became bolder, I would knock on the door and invite them to come to our church. Now, of course, this was better than doing nothing, but still I did not see people saved. I kept on witnessing, though, and I also began working with young people. I was fairly successful leading young people to know Christ as their Saviour, but I was not very successful as far as going out and knocking on doors was concerned. My trouble was that I was not using the Word. The Bible says we have to *share the Word*. The

Lord told Peter to go to Cornelius's household and tell them *words* whereby he and all his house should be saved (Acts 11:14). Unless we share the Word of Life, we are not going to be very successful at it.

I was really in earnest, wanting to know how to witness, but I didn't have a plan. A salesman has a plan of what he is going to do before he goes out to sell. I didn't have a plan, so God finally put me with a man who knew something about witnessing. I watched him when he entered a home to witness. He talked to them about the Lord. He told them what the Lord meant to him. But he also took the Bible and opened it, and showed them scriptures on how they could be saved. And he was a soul-winner! The Lord began to teach me those things. I began to take the Bible and show folk how to be saved from the Scriptures. I began to see people saved!

The first few years, I was winning approximately three people a year to the Lord. Later on, this number increased, but I wasn't giving a lot of time to soul-winning. We have to have priorities. A lady who goes to get her hair fixed each week, usually has an appointment and goes at that time. We should set aside a certain amount of time each week for witnessing. Of course, we should also witness each time we have an opportunity. But we should set aside a specific time each week to go out into the community and witness.

As I improved in my witnessing and soul-winning, I began to work in a State-wide youth work for the Baptists. One weekend I was going to Memphis, Tennessee, for a State training program. A man called and asked if I would mind picking up a man in Etowah and take him along with me to Memphis. I told him I would be glad to and went to pick him up. When I met Dale Smith at a service station in Etowah, he was witnessing to a man. I thought I was a pretty good witness, but I just didn't witness to people while they were pumping gas into my gas tank. I didn't witness to people on the street. But Dale did. There was a young man there having car trouble, so Dale invited him to ride with us. While we were on the way, Dale sat in the back seat and talked with him about Jesus all the way to Athens.

While we were in Memphis for the weekend for the youth training program, I picked up immediately that Dale was not like the other men there. While we were eating lunch, Dale was sitting with the young people who were going to college there, and was witnessing to them about Jesus. Wherever he came in contact with people, he witnessed to them. I had never met a man like this. I had never met a man who witnessed to everyone he met. And he did it in a way that did not offend them. He did it in love and humility.

That week my eyes were opened regarding witnessing. God was teaching me something. He was teaching me how to witness. He was training me by letting me watch someone else who knew how to be an effective witness. Everywhere Dale went, he would tell what Jesus meant to him, and what He could mean to them, and he would give out tracts.

I began to do what I saw him do. At first, it wasn't easy. It took me a while to get bold enough to do this. But little by little, I did, and to my amazement, I began to see people saved. I began to see people saved as they were pumping gas into my gas tank. I would ask them, "Do you know Christ as your Saviour?"

If they would say, "No, I don't," I would ask if they had a few minutes so I could talk to them. Sometimes they would say Yes. Sometimes they would say No. But many times I have talked to people about Jesus and just led them right into accepting Christ as their Saviour.

One night I was in a soul-winning seminar in Gadsen,

Alabama, and I was going back to the hotel. I had witnessed to about every person in the hotel where I was staying. They had one of those elevators that you can stop anywhere you want to. There was a colored elevator boy who was taking me up to the room. I asked him if he knew Jesus as his Saviour. The minute I said that, tears came into his eyes. He said, "No, I don't, but I would like to," and so I told him to stop the elevator. I took out my New Testament, and I showed him the *Roman's Road* on how to be saved. He accepted Christ gladly into his heart. People are dying for someone to come and show them how to be saved.

One time I was in Florida helping with a lay revival. I went to eight or ten houses from the church and knocked on the doors and told the people that we were from the First Baptist Church. I told them we were having a lay revival and would like to come in and talk to them. At one house where they invited us in, we found a man dying of tuberculosis. He didn't know Jesus as his Saviour. He was 62 years old, and he had lived there all his life, and no one had come and told him how to be saved. He had been invited to come to church, but no one took time to explain to him from God's Word what he must do to be saved. That day I explained to him the way of salvation, using the Bible. He gladly received Christ as his Saviour.

I never get on an airplane unless I ask Jesus to place me beside someone for me to witness to. You would be surprised, if you are available, what He will do through you!

One time I was in Mississippi in a meeting, teaching soul-winning in a church. When I got through, I was supposed to go to Alabama and hold some more meetings, but I told Norvel Hayes, whom I was working with at that time, that the Lord wanted me to go back to Athens, Tennessee, where I had been invited to work in a lay revival. A friend of mine was to take me to the plane. We got my things together and got in the car. But on the way to the airport, I remember I felt led to stop at a house and witness. It was a little yellow house, and I stopped and asked them if they knew the Lord. They said they did, but they had some next-door neighbors who didn't. So we went next door and witnessed to these people. Both of them were saved!

We got to the airport on time, and I asked the Lord to put someone next to me on the plane that I could witness to. He put a man next to me who was really mixed up in his beliefs. He had been going to a church that didn't believe in the blood of Christ and its atoning power. They really didn't believe in a lot of things, and I had a chance to talk with him and share with him. I got off the plane in Atlanta, Georgia, and went into the snack bar to get something to eat. All of the seats were taken except in a booth where two colored men were sitting. I sat down there and began to talk to them. I told them about Jesus, and both of them got under conviction. If I'd had the time, I could have won them to the Lord, but their airplane was leaving, so I gave them a tract and prayed for them.

Then I flew into Chattanooga and went on to Athens and spoke there on a Thursday night. After I spoke, several people came forward to make decisions for Christ. Then, on Sunday morning they sent me out to speak at a mission. We had seven people saved that morning in the service.

So you can see what God will do if you are available. God spoke to me in Mississippi and told me to come back to within 25 miles of my home, and you see what He did! Many souls were saved that weekend because I was obedient to Christ. Obedience is better than sacrifice.

Because of lack of training, I had to learn to witness the hard way. A lot of the trial and error can be taken out of it. Our churches should have training programs to train their members to be successful witnesses and soul-winners. Just as salesmen are trained in the best techniques, we need to be trained. We need schools on evangelism. No training or technique is an end in itself, of course. The Holy Spirit must take what we present and make it real to the person we are witnessing to. It is the Holy Spirit's responsibility to make Jesus real, and He will do that if we go out prayerfully and realize that we are just a tool that the Lord is working through, and that it is *HIS* work, not ours.

Jesus Commands Us to Witness

"But ye shall receive power, after that the Holy Ghost is come upon you: and ye shall be witnesses unto me both in Jerusalem, and in all Judaea, and in Samaria, and unto the uttermost part of the earth" (Acts 1:8).

In the above words we see Jesus as many Christians have never seen Him—the commanding Christ.

"Ye are my friends, if ye do whatsoever I COMMAND you" (John 15:14). "These things I COMMAND you, that ye love one another" (John 15:17). "As the Father gave me COMMANDMENT, even so I do" (John 14:31). "This is my COMMANDMENT, that ye love one another, as I have loved you" (John 15:12). "He COMMANDETH even the winds and water, and they obey Him" (Luke 8:25). "And the times of this ignorance, God winked at; but now COMMANDETH men everywhere to repent" (Acts 17:30).

Jesus *commands* us to be witnesses. It is not something we can choose to do or choose not to do. God wants every born-again Christian to learn how to witness successfully, and He has *commanded* us to do this. So, are we going to do it, or are we going to be disobedient Christians? The normal Christian life is a witnessing life. In Matthew 28:19-20, God has *commanded* us to be witnesses. Could the reason why so many Christians do not have power, joy, and real victory in their lives be that they are disobedient to the command of God?

We learn by doing. After instruction, the Christian needs to learn how to win the lost by going out and witnessing. How do people learn to ride a bicycle? Do they learn to ride a bicycle by playing football? Of course not! How does a person learn to play the piano? Not by buying sheets of music. Not by just manipulating the piano keys. How do people learn to swim? They don't learn to swim by driving an automobile. Not by talking about it, *but by doing something about it.*

All these above-mentioned things can be self-taught. There are many people who teach themselves to play an instrument, or drive a car, etc. But in most cases, they learn quicker and better by having instruction. So it is with witnessing and soul-winning. We can teach ourselves by studying the Word and by doing. With God's help, many have become great soul-winners this way. And as with anything, practice makes perfect.

It is also true that we are all born with different talents. Some seem to have a natural talent for music, some for mechanics, some for science, etc. And some seem to have a natural talent for witnessing. It comes natural for them to talk to people, to be convincing, to have a way of showing a genuine interest and concern for others. For those of us who do not seem to be endowed in this way, let us not let that keep us from being good witnesses, too. We might have to work a little harder at it, or it might take us a little longer to be able to do it well, but by God's grace, we *will.* God expects no more than our best, but He does expect our best.

One time an evangelist spoke to a men's prayer and Bible study group about witnessing. The leader said, "We can't do that. We are not deep enough in God."

32

When the evangelist asked if they had been meeting and studying the Bible, the leader said they had just been studying for two years. That is the attitude of most people. They think one has to be a Bible scholar to be a witness and a soul-winner. This is not true.

Billy Graham says that the sad fact of the matter is that some of our greatest Bible scholars are our poorest soul-winners. I have trained 12-year-old children to witness in evangelism schools. They have gone out after one week's time in school, sharing Christ with other people, and winning people to the Lord. It is not the Bible scholars who are going to get people saved. They can, if they want to, but being a Bible scholar is not the criteria. You just have to be *willing*.

One time I was waiting before the Lord. The Lord had been dealing with me about teaching soul-winning for Southern Baptists in Tennessee. I said, "Lord, I don't have the ability. Lord, I just don't have the ability to do this."

And the Lord said to me, "Son, I don't need your ability, but your availability."

"Are you available?" If you are available to tell others about Christ and get up each morning and say, "Lord, I am available to go where you want me to go, and do what you want me to do, and say what you want me to say, after you get me there," and just be a vessel that He can work through, it will change your life completely. God will bring people across your path that need to be saved.

Not long ago, I was in the hospital talking to a lady about the Lord. She knew Christ as her Saviour, and while I was talking to her, a man overheard our conversation. The next day, I went back to see this lady, and she said, "Jimmy, go over to the next room and speak to that young man. He heard us talking about Jesus yesterday, and he said he wanted to talk to you."

33

So I talked to the young man. He asked if I was a preacher. I told him I was a layman. He said, "Well, I heard you talking about Jesus, and you sounded like you knew Him."

I said, "I do know Him."

He said, "Would you mind sharing with me about Jesus?"

I shared with him about the Lord and what the Lord had done for me. As I took my Bible and shared with him the words of life, that man accepted Christ as his Saviour. When you make yourself available, and you go armed with just a few simple scriptures on how to lead people to Christ, God will bring lost people across your path. Until soul-winning becomes the business of our lives, we will not lead many people from darkness to light.

Soul-winning is a great art. We should study it carefully. Study the lives and methods of other great soul-winners! We should never get so hung up on books that we forget the Bible. The Bible is the Book of books! Soul-winning is the world's greatest business proposition. Think what it can mean! You can be a partner with Jesus in leading others to Him, taking men out of the hands of the enemy, out of bondage, out of failure, out of weakness, and introducing them to Jesus who will give them strength, joy, and success. We are offering them the greatest thing in the world. It brings the greatest joy, the greatest success, and it pays the greatest dividends. The joy that it gives to the one who finds Christ, the blessings that go into that home, can never be estimated.

We might win one man to Christ, and that man might, in turn, lead many, many others to Christ. I have led men to Christ who were alcoholics, dope addicts, and later on have gotten the report that those men were preaching the gospel. You see, we never know what is going to happen. We can never estimate the amount of success we are going to have from the words that we say.

Our time is not our own. Every moment and every unsaved man are golden opportunities. You are giving the greatest blessing, and the price is their confession of the Lordship of the Lord Jesus, and that they would accept Him as their Saviour. God loves these people, and He wants to reach them through us. He tells us—GO!

Sometimes Jesus *commands* us to do something we do not want to do. I have always taught others to witness in love, and I believe in 99 percent of the time we should witness in love and be gentle and kind. But sometimes Jesus has something else in mind. Some people have to be shocked into the realization that if they do not give their lives to God they are going to hell.

One day I was sweeping the sidewalk of my business in Riceville, Tennessee. I was just minding my own business when the word of the Lord came to me saying, "Do you see that man over there?"

I had not seen anyone, but I turned and looked. I saw an elderly man sitting on the ground under a tree whittling on a stick.

The Lord said, "Go tell that man that I have been patient with him for years and have spared his life many times, but he continues to reject me. Tell him that he has been walking on the brink of hell, and unless he accepts Me as his Saviour, he is going there soon."

Let me make this clear. Never go and tell someone something like this unless you are certain the Lord has spoken to you to do so.

I said, "Lord, I do not want to do this." But I had hardly spoken three words before he said for me to go and tell him. And believe me, He meant business.

So I went over to this man and said, "Sir, I was just sweeping my sidewalk, and the Lord Jesus spoke to me and gave me a message for you." I repeated what

35

the Lord had told me to tell him.

Before I had completed giving him the message, he began to cry. I told him to kneel with me and I would lead him in a prayer to accept Jesus as his Saviour. He prayed the sinner's prayer, and he accepted Jesus as his Saviour. Praise God! I found out later this man had nearly been killed in a car wreck just a few weeks before. But God is so good. He spared his life. I also found out he had a heart condition. God knew just what it would take to get him to accept Him as his Saviour.

We need to be obedient when God speaks. When He *commands,* we should obey!

Once I was teaching soul-winning in a church and we were getting ready to go from house to house witnessing. The pastor of that church told me about a woman who practiced witchcraft and wanted to know if I would go and visit her. He said others had been there but always had a bad reception. She would curse them, and tell them to get off her property. I told him that I would be glad for the opportunity of going and telling her about Jesus. You see, some would be afraid to go near a person like her, but God does not want you to be fearful because He does not give us the spirit of fear—but love and power, and a sound mind.

To go and witness to someone like this, you have to know who you are in Christ Jesus and what you can do as a result of it. I asked two other persons to go with me so I would have someone to back me up in prayer as I was witnessing to her. We held hands and we broke the power of the devil. We bound up the cursing spirits, the spirit of witchcraft, and any other spirits that would hinder our witness. We claimed her soul for Jesus and told the devil to take his hands off of her. We prayed the prayer of faith, believing what we prayed would come to pass (Mark 11:24).

36

We witnessed to her of the saving grace of the Lord Jesus Christ. We told her that Satan was deceiving her, and would take her soul to hell. We were telling her these things but we were witnessing in love. We told her we loved her, and that Christ died for her sins, and was ready to forgive her and save her.

Now everyone else who had been there had had trouble, but you see, we bound up these powers of darkness in faith. We had a wonderful time witnessing to her and she was nice to us and listened to us. She did not accept Jesus as her Saviour that day. I kept praying for her when the Lord would bring her to my memory and I would confess that she would be saved. About a year or so later, I received a message that she was saved, and also her whole family and they are going to church. PRAISE GOD, IS ANYTHING TOO HARD FOR HIM? NO, NO, NO,— A THOUSAND TIMES, NO, FOR GOD IS GOD AND CAN DO ANYTHING, IF WE ONLY HAVE FAITH.

Fishers of Men

(Some quotations in this chapter were taken from Lester Sumrall's book, *Fishers of Men*.)

"Now as he walked by the sea of Galilee, he saw Simon and Andrew his brother casting a net into the sea: for they were fishers. And Jesus said unto them, Come ye after me, and I will make you to become fishers of men. And straightway they forsook their nets, and followed him" (Mark 1:16-18).

The speaker above was Christ. He addressed Simon and Andrew and told them to come and follow Him, and He would make them to become fishers of men. In Luke 5:10-11, James and John also forsook all and followed Him: "And so was also James and John, the sons of Zebedee, which were partners with Simon. And Jesus said unto Simon, Fear not; from henceforth thou shalt catch men. And when they had brought their ships to land, they forsook all, and followed him."

Jesus was not only addressing those men of that day, but He is also talking to you and me, and everyone who would be his disciple. He wants us to go and catch men.

The disciples didn't become fishers of men instantly. Jesus began to train them. You and I need to be trained so we can go out and catch men. The man who does not go fishing is not going to catch fish. Neither will we win souls unless we put forth an effort to go forth and witness.

We learn to be fishers of men by fishing for men. No man ever caught a fish while going hunting. No one has ever caught fish while playing golf. We must be about our Father's business. If we are to catch fish, we must go where there are some fish. If the unsaved don't come to church, we have to go where they are to witness to them. We must cast out a line, and we must have proper bait.

In sports magazines, such as *Field and Stream*, we can read stories about fishing. We can learn all about where and when to catch the different varieties of fish. Perhaps we know just the right kind of bait to use and the right kind of fishing rod. But unless we go fishing, we'll never catch any fish. Likewise, we can read about following Jesus. We can read about fishing for men. We can know all about soul-winning and witnessing, but unless we obey Christ's command to follow Him and put our know-how into practice, we'll never catch any men.

Let's look at Andrew and see if he was a good fisherman. In John 1:35-42, we read: "Again the next day after John stood, and two of his disciples; and looking upon Jesus as he walked, he saith, Behold the Lamb of God! And the two disciples heard him speak, and they followed Jesus. Then Jesus turned, and saw them following, and saith unto them, What seek ye? They said unto him, Rabbi, (Which is to say, being interpreted, Master) where dwellest thou? He saith unto them, Come and see. They came and saw where he dwelt, and abode with him that day: for it was about the tenth hour. One of the two which heard John speak, and followed him, was Andrew, Simon Peter's brother. He first findeth his own brother, Simon, and saith unto him, We have found the Messias, which is, being interpreted, the Christ. And he brought him to Jesus. And when Jesus beheld him, he said, Thou art Simon, the son of Jona: thou shalt be called Cephas, which is by interpretation, a stone."

We see from the Scriptures that Andrew was a fisherman, and probably his father before him was a fisherman. From boyhood, Andrew probably watched the boats come in and go out. He probably helped unload the fish and did what he could to help his father. He accepted his vocation as a fisherman. But after meeting Jesus, his entire life experienced a remarkable change. He decided, when the call came to him, to quit fishing for fish and become a fisher of men. As a result of accepting Christ, he went and told his brother, Peter, about Jesus, and Peter came and accepted Christ.

Andrew is a perfect example of what a witness should be. He brought his brother to Jesus. We see Andrew catch fish one by one. He brought his brother to Jesus, but his brother caught fish in multitudes. The first message Peter preached on the day of Pentecost, thousands were saved. There are not many people on earth today who can preach a message and thousands be saved. But there are many thousands and even millions of Christians who could reach a few for Jesus. And perhaps the one you win, will go out and win multitudes. We might not have the call of God on our lives to be an evangelist or to go to a far country to be a missionary, but we can win souls for Christ one by one like Andrew.

"Cast thy bread upon the waters; for thou shalt find it after many days" (Eccles. 11:1).

A woman had been praying for years: "Lord, I would like to be a missionary to a far country." But yet she had not been a missionary at home. One day while she was kneeling and praying, the Lord spoke to her: "You have not been faithful in the little things I gave you to do. Therefore, how can I use you to do greater things? What about the people who live next door to you? Have you ever witnessed to them about me? There are people all around you who are lost. Have you ever witnessed to them

40

about my saving grace?"

The woman, of course, was very sad as she had failed to do what Christ has commanded all Christians to do—to be a witness wherever we are. In the barber shop, at the supermarket, anywhere we are, to share Christ, to tell people about His saving grace. We get our eyes on big ministries or on going somewhere, or doing something that takes us to a far land. Yet we all have a ministry at home, to be home missionaries, and preach the gospel of Jesus Christ to those who are all around us.

We need to be like Andrew. He was an example of what we should be. He went out and found his brother. We should all be able to go out and win ONE to Christ. Many Christians do not have the ability to preach. They do not have the ability to write songs, and they do not have the ability to sing. They feel like they are not qualified to work for Christ. They might say, "We feel useless and worthless."

This is the wrong attitude. The devil, himself, is the one who causes such feelings, because he is a supernatural power of false suggestion. If we cannot preach like Peter or Paul, like Billy Graham or Oral Roberts, or other great men; if we cannot sing like David, or other great singers of our time, we can still tell someone about Christ. If nothing else, we can give our personal testimony of what Christ has done for us. We can go out like Andrew and fish for men *one at a time.* Others may catch the multitudes, but we can catch a few. You might feel like you cannot do much, but remember, God does not need your ability. He needs your availability. Are you available to go and witness? To go and tell people about Jesus? The greatest thing a human being can do is bring another person to know Jesus Christ as his Saviour.

Saving souls was the life passion of Jesus. The redemption of a poor sinner was more important to Him than the glory He had with God before the world was, for He emptied Himself of it all. It meant more to Him than the joys of heaven, for He left those joys to become a man of many sorrows. It meant more to Him than life. He gave His life a ransom for you and me. It meant more to Him than occupying heaven's throne, for He left that throne to die on the cross for lost sinners that through Him they could be saved. He gave it all up that we through faith might become the sons of God. Soul-saving was the only business big enough to bring Jesus out of the palaces of heaven to a world of woe and wickedness. It was the only reality significant enough to bring Jesus down from glory, from the honors of heaven, to the depths of humanity to die a terrible death of a common criminal between two malefactors. Do not forget, Christ came to earth to seek and to save that which was lost. To seek and save the lost is the biggest job in the world. Remember, "He which converteth a sinner from the error of his ways, shall save a soul from death" (James 5:20).

Jesus made saving souls His business. We must also make this our business. If we will go forth, will be willing to use the authority that Jesus has given us, we, too, will see many people come to know Christ as Saviour.

We have great authority in the name of Jesus. When I go out witnessing, I always bind up the powers of darkness. I always come against Satan in the Name of Jesus and plead the blood of Jesus. Jesus said in Matthew 18:18, "Verily I say unto you, whatsoever ye shall bind on earth shall be bound in heaven, and whatsoever ye shall loose on earth shall be loosed in heaven." We have binding authority, or you might say that we have binding power so that we can bind the powers of the darkness of this world.

One of the promises of Jesus is found in John 14:12-14, " Verily, verily, I say unto you, He that believeth on me, the works that I do shall he do also; and greater works

42

than these shall he do; because I go unto my Father. And whatsoever ye shall ask in my name, that will I do, that the Father may be glorified in the Son. If ye shall ask any thing in my name, I will do it." His promise is that if we ask *anything* in His name, He will do it. But, of course, we must ask in faith, believing, and if we realize who we are in Christ and the authority we have in Christ, we will go out and bind the powers of darkness. We are not fighting a battle against flesh and blood, but against spiritual forces. "For we wrestle not against flesh and blood, but against principalities, against powers, against the rulers of the darkness of this world, against spiritual wickedness in high places" (Ephes. 6:12).

I have been in churches conducting soul-winning seminars, and they would have names of people who were violent, or mean, and ask me if I would go visit these people. I would get someone to go with me, and before we got there we would stop and bind the powers of Satan, the powers of darkness, and the cursing spirits, in the Name of Jesus, and plead the blood. Many, many times we would go places where people were practicing the occult and all kinds of wicked things. Other people had been there time and time again and been thrown out, and cursed. But when we would bind these powers, we would have a nice visit. I have had the privilege of leading many of them to know Jesus Christ as their Saviour.

When we go out fishing for men, let's go in the Name of Jesus, using the *authority* that Christ has given us. Let's expect great miracles. The greatest miracle of all is when a soul is saved. We cannot save them, but let's bring them to Jesus who can!

43

Sowing Seeds

" In the mean while his disciples prayed him, saying, Master, eat. But he said unto them, I have meat to eat that ye know not of. Therefore said the disciples one to another, Hath any man brought him aught to eat? Jesus saith unto them, My meat is to do the will of him that sent me, and to finish his work. Say not ye, There are yet four months, and then cometh harvest? behold, I say unto you, Lift up your eyes, and look on the fields; for they are white already to harvest" (John 4:31-35).

Unless we sow seed, we'll never have a harvest. God has to have someone to sow the seed. He did not command that we go out and win souls. He commanded that we be witnesses—that we sow the seed. There are many people who, more or less, sow the seed, while others come and water the seed, and others come and win the souls to Christ. Sometimes a farmer sows seed and is also a partaker. He gets to gather in the harvest, also. But there are others who just sow seed.

"And he that reapeth receiveth wages, and gathereth fruit unto life eternal: that both he that soweth and he that reapeth may rejoice together. And herein is that saying true, One soweth, and another reapeth. I sent you to reap that whereon ye bestowed no labour: other men laboured, and ye are entered into their labours" (John 4:36-38).

The tract ministry is a seed-sowing ministry. We, as Christians, should never go anywhere without tracts in our pockets. The ladies should always have tracts in their handbags. We should dedicate our shirt pockets, as men, to the Lord. We never know when we might hand out a tract to a desperate person and they might read it and be saved. Many people will tell you that this is useless because a lot of tracts are just thrown away. Well, so what! If a thousand tracts are handed out and only five persons come to know Jesus, or even only one person comes to know Him through the tract, it is worthwhile. We know many tracts are going to be thrown away and not read, but many of them will be. We never know what good is being done when we pass out tracts. Tracts are a very important ministry!

In my business, for years, I put tracts in people's bags as I was bagging up their merchandise. I was in the gift business, and I kept thousands of tracts on hand. I would put tracts in their bags for a long time. I didn't hear any results, and I wondered whether or not it was being very fruitful. Finally I began to get some answers from it. A truck driver came into my place of business one night and bought some gifts. I talked to him a bit about Jesus, and I put a tract in his bag. In just a few days, I got a report that this man had accepted Christ as his Saviour. So, let's be faithful to sow the seed. One will sow, another will water, and another will reap the harvest. Without the sowing, there would be no reaping.

One time I was going to West Virginia to work in a lay revival. We would usually go on Wednesdays and come back on Sundays. West Virginia is a place that needs much work done in it, as most places today. Christian America is not so Christian. There is plenty of missionary work that needs to be done right here at home. About 75 percent of the people there are lost. We had about 20 men out there working in a revival, and I was just helping. A friend of mine from Cleveland, Tennessee, was conducting the revival. All week long I worked hard. I went out and witnessed every day, and I didn't see anyone saved. I was sowing seed and counseling with people and helping them, but I wasn't seeing anyone saved. Almost everybody had won someone to Christ, except me.

Friday night came, and I was depressed. After the meeting that night, I went to the bowling alley. I just wanted to see someone saved so bad. I didn't see anyone at the bowling alley to witness to, so I went to a washateria. (Do you know that washaterias are wonderful places to witness? While people are washing their clothes, they have nothing to do, and they will be glad to talk with you about Jesus.) So, I went to the washateria, but there wasn't anyone in there. I finally gave up and went to my room.

When I got to my room it was about midnight. I began to pray. I prayed for about two hours and asked God, "God, why have I driven all this distance at my own expense, and I haven't seen anyone saved?" Usually when I would go on these lay revivals I would see several people saved. I was concerned and kept asking God *why* I hadn't seen any results this time.

Then the word of the Lord came to me, saying, "Jimmy, aren't you willing to be just a seed-sower?"

It was plain that I wasn't, so I said, "Lord, no! I am not willing just to be a seed-sower." You see, you have to be honest with God, and He knew my heart, anyway.

But He said, "Jimmy, I must have people to sow the seed because unless the seed is sown, there will be no harvest."

Many times people's hearts are not ready to accept

46

the seed, so all we can do is sow. After the seed is planted in their hearts and is watered, it begins to germinate and bring forth life everlasting.

I told the Lord I would try to be patient enough to sow seeds, and that I was willing to be willing to be a seed-sower. The Lord is so good! He knows when we need lifting up.

The next morning we met for breakfast. The laymen from the church and the laymen who were working the revival were sharing some of what happened the day before. A man told about some people he had had on his heart for some time who were lost. All these people, he said, were over 60 years old and hard cases.

The Lord spoke to me and said, "Jimmy, you go with him."

You would really have had to be with us to realize what hard cases these people were in the natural. There are two worlds out there—the natural and the supernatural. In ourselves, we can do nothing, but in Christ we can do all things. We went to these people's homes. Five of them had never accepted Christ as Saviour. One was a backslider.

Many times before, people had been there sowing seeds, but there had never been any interest shown in accepting Christ as Saviour. This time we bound the power of Satan as we went and asked God's power to work on these people. And it was so beautiful! PRAISE THE LIVING GOD FOREVERMORE!

We began to share about Jesus. The power of God convicted them of their sins, and tears streamed down their faces. One after another accepted Christ. We were gone only two and a half hours that morning, and six people accepted Jesus Christ as their Saviour—all of them hard cases, over 60 years old.

If we will only believe, all these things can be done to

47

the glory of God. I have witnessed to many people who were supposedly impossible cases. With man, it is impossible, but with God all things are possible.

We are saved by faith. We are healed by faith. And we need faith for winning souls. Before we go witnessing, we must pray and ask God to lead us to the right people. We must believe that He is a rewarder of those who diligently seek Him. We must believe that we have power with God, and we must have faith to believe that good will come out of our witnessing. I have witnessed for a whole week and never seen anybody saved, but I was sowing seed. The Lord showed me this. Sometimes I have just sown seed and sown seed and sown seed. But then I have gone out and led as many as fourteen people to the Lord in perhaps two hours.

I was teaching soul-winning in a church in Pennsylvania. When it came time to go witnessing, no one from the church showed up, so some of my friends went along. We did not know where to go since we were strangers in that city. We began by witnessing on the streets. After witnessing for a while, I could see that we were not doing much good. I prayed for a plan, and the Lord spoke to me and told us to go to the shopping center.

We did not know where a shopping center was, but we asked someone. There were three shopping centers, but only one had a mall. This was Easter weekend, and there were a lot of young people out of school. Since they like to lull around a mall, we went there.

We began to pass out tracts and witness, each going our own way. First I saw two young girls talking outside the mall. I began to talk to them, and they accepted Jesus as their Saviour with tears running down their faces. Then I began to witness to some boys hanging around. They in turn began to holler at other young people and say, "Come over here. There is a Jesus-man preaching to us."

They started off by just jesting and making fun of me, but it did not matter. I just kept talking to them about Jesus. Soon I had probably eighteen young people listening to me. I knew some of them were making fun, and I asked the Lord to move those off who were not interested. In just a few minutes I had only fourteen boys and girls. This was outside the mall. Twelve of these bowed their heads and prayed the sinner's prayer with me, many of them crying as the Lord Jesus came into their hearts. Praise God forevermore for His goodness!

But you see, there had been someone in front of me sowing the seed. Someone had watered the seed, and now the harvest was prepared. They were ready to hear the word and accept Christ as Saviour. We must not get discouraged when we go out witnessing and no one responds and accepts the Lord. We are lifting up Jesus, and we are fulfilling the command of Christ to witness.

Successful witnessing is simply sharing Christ in the power of the Holy Spirit and leaving the results to God. We must leave the results to God! God, and God alone, can give the increase!

"In the morning sow thy seed, and in the evening withhold not thine hand: for thou knowest not whether shall prosper, either this or that, or whether they both shall be alike good" (Eccles. 11:6).

He that Winneth Souls
is Wise

"The fruit of the righteous is a tree of life; and he that winneth souls is wise" (Prov. 11:30).

If you would be wise, you would begin to witness and win souls to Christ. We need to be about our Father's business. Our Father's business is for people to know Him. He is in the soul-saving business. The devil delights in getting us so preoccupied with "things" that we have little or no time to witness. So many things that we spend so much time on are going to seem so insignificant and worthless in eternity, and we will regret that we didn't have our priorities right. We should have been busy laying up treasures in heaven instead of fooling our time away with cares of this life.

You might say, "Who should I witness to?" We can witness to the people we come in contact with every day. The people we work with. . . the people at the grocery store. . . our barber. . . our neighbors. . . the teller at the bank.

Many years ago, I was in the grocery business, and I would witness to people who came into the store. I had a man come to me and tell me, "Jimmy, I feel I should warn you about something. If you don't quit witnessing so much in your business, you are going to drive customers away from your store."

I said, "Brother, this business belongs to God, and His business is winning souls. We should make it our business, too. Therefore. I am going to witness for Christ Jesus, and if I lose customers because of it, then I'll just have to lose customers. I don't depend upon this business for a living, because this business is not my source of supply. God is!"

My Father, who is in Heaven, is my source of supply. He said He would supply all my needs according to His riches in glory. He said, "Seek ye first the kingdom of God and His righteousness, and all these things shall be added unto you" (Matt. 6:33). I appreciated this man's concern, but as long as I live, I am going to be a witnessing Christian. It did not hurt my business. On the contrary, my business was successful.

One of the best years we had had in the gift business was 1973. That year I was in my place of business about 75 percent of the time. But in 1974, I left my business in the hands of people who could operate it while I went out on the road for Christ. I was in full-time ministry, teaching soul-winning, teaching seminars on faith, healing, etc. I wasn't at my place of business over three weeks. I doubt if I worked 21 days all year. But every day I would get up and say, "Thank you, Lord, because my business is successful. Thank you, Lord, because I am seeking first the Kingdom of God and your righteousness, and you are taking care of my business! I bind the power of Satan away from my business and protect it from any attacks of the enemy."

I went about my business of working for the Lord and winning souls. In 1974, I led around 200 people to know Christ as Saviour. In all kinds of situations, on buses, in elevators, in hotels, in motels, and on the streets. There were all kinds of people, drunkards, bootleggers,

51

prostitutes, moral people, young and old.

And my gift business doubled! The reason was that I sought the Kingdom of God first. I believe what the Bible says, "Beloved, I wish above all things that thou mayest prosper and be in health, even as thy soul prospereth" (III John 2). PRAISE THE LIVING GOD FOREVERMORE! If we are prospering for God, if our souls are prospering, we will not have to worry about sickness, or finances, or anything else.

Daniel tells us in Chapter 12:3, "And they that be wise shall shine as the brightness of the firmament; and they that turn many to righteousness as the stars for ever and ever." Do you want to be wise? Then begin to share with others what Christ has done for you, and lead people out of darkness into His marvelous light.

Last year I taught witnessing seminars all over the United States. I was in a Full Gospel Church which really seemed on fire for God from all outward appearances. They had a wonderful time when they came together. The services were very good. They had a wonderful praise time and worship time. God was blessing, and people were being healed in the services. Everything looked real good. I asked the pastor, "How many souls did you baptize last year?" This church had about 200 members.

He said, "Well, I am ashamed to say that we just baptized fifteen people."

A lot of Full Gospel people are missing God. They are missing God because they are moving with God in healing, in miracles, in praise, and in worship. But they are not moving with God in salvation. This has been my experience in most of the Full Gospel Churches I have been to. Not very many of them have a visitation program. Not very many of them have an outreach program to go out and witness to people that are lost. On the other hand, we have the other denominations who witness to people

52

who are lost, but they have no program whereby people can be healed. They never have any miracles in their churches. There are never any cripples who walk off, and there never will be any cripples walk off as long as they believe in salvation only.

If you want to move with God in salvation, He will let you move with Him in salvation. There are many denominations that don't believe in healing. They don't believe in miracles. They believe strictly in salvation. Therefore, they see people saved, because they believe in salvation. But that is all they see. What you believe is what you receive, as long as you are believing scriptural things. Salvation is the most important thing, and God wants us to believe for that. But He also wants us to believe for healing and miracles, etc. However, let us not emphasize healing and miracles and neglect salvation.

When I teach soul-winning, I teach in the mornings from 10 to 12, and then we go out and witness in the afternoons. In a Full Gospel Church in one of our Northern cities, I went out witnessing one afternoon. No one from the church had shown up, so my friend and I went out alone. We knocked on a door where the lady happened to attend the church where we were teaching soul-winning. I told her we had come to share Jesus with her, and she said, "I know all about Jesus, Praise the Lord!"

When you are witnessing, you learn to be a good detective and try to trace down leads to get names of lost people, so I asked her if her next-door neighbor knew Jesus. She said she didn't know. I asked about the neighbor on the other side of her, and she said she was ashamed to say that she didn't know that, either. I asked her how long she had lived there, and she said she had lived there two years. I said, "You have lived here two years, and you don't know whether your neighbors are lost or not?"

She said, "No, no! I don't."

Here we have an example of many people who say they are Christians. They say they love God, but they are not obeying Him. He said, "Ye shall be my witnesses." We find in Ezekiel 33:8; "When I say unto the wicked, O, wicked man, thou shalt surely die; if thou dost not speak to warn the wicked from his way, that wicked man shall die in his iniquity; but his blood will I require at thine hand."

You see, my friend, unless we warn people whom we come in contact with about the wrath of God, unless we tell them about Jesus, their blood on the day of judgment will be required of our hands. We will stand before Jesus on the day of judgment, and He will say, "Why did you not tell that person about me?" He said, "If you deny me before men, I will deny you before my Father which is in heaven, but if you will confess me before men, I will confess you before my Father, which is in Heaven."

One thing that is wrong with people who don't witness is that they are ashamed of the Gospel. They say they are not ashamed, but they really are. Paul said, "I am not ashamed of the Gospel of the Lord Jesus Christ, for it is the power of God unto salvation" (Rom. 1:16). We must not be ashamed of the Gospel. We have to go forth and tell people words whereby they can be saved.

Let's be wise! Let's start winning souls! Get a little training, and go out and witness. A person who says, "I cannot do it," is defeated before he starts. Don't wait until you become more scientific in your methods. Waiting to become an efficient worker is like waiting to be saved. It is like a person saying he cannot go into the water until he learns to swim.

Efficiency is the result of experience. Experience is the best teacher. Although one is not experienced when he begins, people will respect and respond to one who brings him a positive, simple, and honest, concerned effort to

54

show them Christ as Saviour. Many inexperienced young people have been honored by God, regardless of experience. Our aim should be to win souls for Christ at every given opportunity.

Bearing Fruit

"And on the morrow, when they were come from Bethany, he was hungry; and seeing a fig tree afar off having leaves, he came, if haply he might find anything thereon: and when he came to it, he found nothing but leaves; for the time of figs was not yet. And Jesus answered and said unto it, No man eat fruit of thee hereafter for ever. And his disciples heard it" (Mark 11:12-14).

"And in the morning, as they passed by, they saw the fig tree dried up from the roots. And Peter calling to remembrance saith unto him, Master, behold, the fig tree which thou cursedst is withered away. And Jesus, answering saith unto them, Have faith in God" (Mark 11:20-22).

Many Christians and many churches remind me of the barren fig tree. We see that Jesus came by the wayside and saw a fig tree in the distance that looked good. The fig tree had plenty of leaves, and it looked as though there was fruit on it. But Jesus went and looked, and there was no fruit. A lot of Christians look like they are bearing fruit. They talk like they are bearing fruit. But I can see Jesus coming into my life and other people's lives looking for fruit and parting the leaves and finding very little or no fruit there.

I want my life to be such that when He parts the

leaves that He will find some fruit—that He will find souls that I have led to Christ. The tree may be very attractive with only leaves, but we need to bear fruit. Are there recorded in heaven names of people that we personally have led to Christ? People that you have taken your Bible and shown them how to be saved? When Jesus comes and He pulls back the leaves of our lives, it is my prayer that He will find fruit.

There is another kind of fruit mentioned in the Bible—the fruit of the Spirit. The fruit of the Spirit is love, joy, peace, long-suffering, gentleness, goodness, faith, meekness, temperance. Christian character is not a mere moral of legal correctness, but it is the manifestation of these nine graces and is produced by the Holy Spirit, not by self-effort. Love, joy, and peace are characteristics of an inward state. Longsuffering, gentleness, and goodness are characteristics in the expression toward man. Faith, meekness, and temperance are characteristics in expression toward God. Taken together, they represent a portrait of Christ.

In the fifteenth chapter of John, Jesus said, " I am the true vine, and my Father is the husbandman. Every branch in me that *beareth not fruit* he taketh away: and every branch that *beareth fruit,* he purgeth it, that it may bring forth *more fruit.* Now, ye are clean through the word which I have spoken unto you. Abide in me, and I in you. As the branch cannot bear fruit of itself, except it abide in the vine; no more can ye, except ye abide in me" (1-4). (Italics mine).

In order to be soul-winners, we have to abide in Him. If we do, we will bear fruit. But He is going to purge us, so we can bring forth *more* fruit. Christ had to purge me from a lot of things. I had a dislike for certain people. God took this away and gave me a deep love for them. Now I witness to them and see them saved. There is an abiding. If we go on to the fifth verse of John 15, we see that "Without me ye can do nothing." How true that is! Without Christ *we can do nothing.*

"If a man abide not in me, he is cast forth as a branch and is withered." We have many Christians that are withered. They are not effective in witnessing. They are not winning souls. They are withered branches without any fruit.

He said, "If ye abide in me, and my words abide in you, ye shall ask what ye will, and it shall be done unto you. Herein is my Father glorified, that ye bear much fruit; so shall ye be my disciples. As the Father hath loved me, so have I loved you: continue ye in my love" (John 15:7-9). That means loving everyone. Jesus loved everyone, and we have to continue in His love. That means loving not only our friends and our family, but the unlovely, the hippies, the alcoholics, the dope addicts, and the prostitutes. It means loving all races and all creeds.

"If ye keep my commandments, ye shall abide in my love; even as I have kept my Father's commandments and abide in His love. These things have I spoken unto you, that my joy might remain in you, and that your joy might be full. This is my commandment, That ye love one another, as I have loved you. . . . Ye are my friends, if ye do whatsoever I command you" (John 15:10-14). He commands us to love one another. He commands us to be witnesses. Are we loving one another? Are we witnessing? Let's purpose in our hearts today, that from this day forward we will hold forth the word of life to those who are lost, and that we will love them and love one another as Christ commanded us. We cannot do this in ourselves, but by His grace and His help, we can.

Remember as we read John 15 that there are three degrees of fruit bearing:

1. Those who bear fruit

2. Those who bring forth more fruit
3. Those who bring forth much fruit

This is also set forth in Matthew 13:23, "But he that received seed into the good ground is he that heareth the word, and understandeth it; which also beareth fruit, and bringeth forth, some an hundredfold, some sixty, some thirty."

We see from these scriptures, that there are degrees of fruit-bearing. Earlier in my Christian life, I would read these scriptures and think how I would love to bring forth a lot of fruit for the Kingdom of God. It was my heart's desire to win souls for Jesus. I wasn't satisfied with just a little fruit. I wanted to bear a lot of fruit.

For years I witnessed and was not very effective in winning souls. At first, I would win three or four people a year to the Lord. I kept working at it and tried to improve myself on my presentation just as a salesman is trained to present his product. I learned by trial and error, since I had no one to teach me.

Finally, I got to the place that I had won about thirty people into the Kingdom of God, and I thought, "If I would only win sixty." So I began to witness more.

You see, you have to give a certain amount of your time to Christ for witnessing. A man who has an appointment to play golf on Saturdays, hardly ever misses playing golf on Saturdays, if that's where his heart is. If your heart is on winning souls, you must set a time to witness. By being faithful and staying on the job and witnessing and passing out tracts, it wasn't but a year or so later that I had reached sixty people for the Lord. Then, I thought, perhaps I could reach 100. But that seemed like just a dream. But by witnessing wherever I was, in the bus stations, on the airplanes, at restaurants, and motels, it wasn't but a few more years till I had reached 100 for Christ. Since then I have led many hundreds to the Lord.

I thought reaching 100 for the Lord was real good until I heard a man speak one night from Louisville, Kentucky. This man told how he witnessed and was winning somewhere like 1,000 people a year to Christ. A thousand a year! I know many Full Gospel Churches who have the signs following that do not win thirty people a year to Christ! And here was a layman winning as high as 1,000 people a year to the Lord all by himself! Fantastic? Yes, it is fantastic! But if you will abide in Christ, and His words abide in you, you, too, will go forth and bear much fruit.

When Jesus was talking about hundredfold, sixty, and thirty, He was using a figure of speech. But we understand that we can bear fruit, and more fruit, and much fruit, if we will make ourselves available. The man who won 1,000 people to the Lord, didn't win them by watching "Gunsmoke," "The Edge of Night," or "Secret Storm." He didn't watch TV two or three hours a night. He did it by putting Christ first because he had a hunger and a burden for lost souls. He works three days a week, and he witnesses four days a week. He speaks all over the world.

Paul tells us in Romans 12:1-2, "I beseech you therefore, brethren, by the mercies of God, that ye present your bodies a living sacrifice, holy, acceptable unto God, which is your reasonable service. And be not conformed to this world: but be ye transformed by the renewing of your mind, that ye may prove what is that good, and acceptable, and perfect, will of God." If we will consecrate our lives to God, He will surely use us and let us bear fruit for eternity. He needs each one of us in His service. Jesus said, "The harvest truly is great, but the laborers are few" (Luke 10:2).

And, my friends, the laborers are not just few, they are very few.

I have been across this country teaching soul-winning. We will have a good crowd come out to the teaching session, but in the doing session when we go out into the streets or from door-to-door, very few people ever show up. Sometimes I have, taught approximately 100 in the morning from 10 to 12. We'll have a break for lunch and have a witnessing session at 2 PM. Maybe five will show up. I have been to churches when no one showed up. Not even the pastor of the church. I have had to go out by myself. "Be not deceived; God is not mocked: for whatsoever a man soweth, that shall he also reap" (Gal. 6:7).

Let's start bearing fruit! When the fruit is first forming, it doesn't look like much, but in time it grows and becomes luscious, a beautiful offering to the Lord, and sustenance and life to the hungry. If you have a desire to bear fruit, God will help you whether it's through sending a teacher to help train you, or just through His Word, or through this book. Then go out in Jesus name and in the power of the Holy Spirit and be His witness. Win souls, and bear fruit for His glory!

Fear

"For God hath not given us the spirit of fear; but of power, and of love, and of a sound mind" (II Tim. 1:7).

Fear is the *number one enemy* of witnessing. God tells us to go into all the world and preach the Gospel, but we don't go as much as we should because of fear.

People often tell me they are afraid to witness. That is from the enemy. The devil puts thoughts in our minds that if we go witnessing, the people will slam the door in our faces, curse us, do this, or do that.

The Bible says, "God does not give us a spirit of fear." Then who does? Satan! When fear comes toward us, we have to rebuke that fear in the Name of Jesus. James 4:7 says, "Resist the devil, and he will flee from you." Jesus has already conquered the devil, and we have the authority in the Name of Jesus to rebuke him, and he will flee. When we do this in faith, the fear will disappear.

Many times when I am teaching soul-winning, I lay my hands on people and rebuke fear and command the spirit of fear to come out of them. I command it to leave, because if they have more than a natural sense of fear, it is a spirit of fear. I John 4:18 tells us that fear has torment. I suppose all of us have been afraid at one time or another. It is a tormenting experience.

Many people agonize with this fear. They really want to speak up for the Lord. They want to get started witnessing and soul-winning. But they have this fear. Rebuke it in Jesus name, and believe God for power to speak for Him!

When I was in bed for seven months, unable to walk, I had the fear I would never walk again. As long as I was bound by fear, I did not get any better. Satan kept telling me: I would never get well, I would never get well, I would never get well. But when I began to believe what the Word said and rebuked fear and commanded it to leave in the Name of Jesus, it did. I got the victory over fear. "Greater is He that is in us than he that is in the world." The devil will try to intimidate us and make us afraid, but quote Scripture to him.

When we realize who we are in Christ, we will begin to take authority over the devil. Not who we are, as John Smith, but who we are in Christ. The Bible plainly tells us that if we are in Christ, we are a new creature (II Cor. 5:17). When we are in Christ, we have the authority He had, because He gave it to us. I John 4:4 says that we are overcomers. Romans 8:37 says we are more than conquerors. We can overcome the world and conquer the devil. As children of God, as sons of God, God has given us power and authority and dominion.

Jesus has commissioned us to go forth in His Name. We cannot do it in ourselves. It is a supernatural commission. We go in His Name. ". . . Go ye into all the world, and preach the gospel to every creature. He that believeth and is baptized shall be saved; but he that believeth not shall be damned" (Mark 16:15-16).

Jesus never asks us to do the impossible. He has commissioned us, as believers, to do this, and He said He would confirm the word with signs following. He has given us power to carry out this commission. We *can* do the works of Christ. We are joint-heirs. We are adopted sons.

63

The Bible says we will be judges and kings and priests. We sit in heavenly places. We are the righteousness of God in Christ, and He has given us power to go out and tear down the devil's stronghold. We should go and not be afraid. Let faith begin to rise, and say, "This is who I am, and I can do all things through Christ which strengtheneth me."

Jesus said, "Whatsoever ye ask the Father in my name, I will do it." This is a most wonderful promise. We can do the asking, and He'll do the doing. Jesus said all authority was given to Him in heaven and on earth. His power is unlimited. Now He challenges you and I to do unlimited asking! He is big enough to do anything you ask Him to do. If you have fear, ask Him to remove the fear. There is no reason for fruitless lives. God wants our lives to be fruitful. When we start believing that God is the reigning Christ, He will take care of His end of the deal. You are a partner with Him *now.* You need not be limited on your end of the partnership, because His company is not limited. He is able to meet the demands, and He is able to undertake anything.

One time when I was working in a revival, some people had a man they wanted me to witness to. This man had thrown everybody out that had ever come to the house to witness before. They asked if I'd be afraid to go. I told them the Greater One lived in me, and that I was not afraid.

I had another man go with me. We bound the power of Satan, and we went in Jesus' Name, believing God. We commanded that this man be freed from Satan, and believed God's power was sufficient to do the job. I knew that I was not sufficient. The man with me knew he was not sufficient. We bound the argumentative spirits. We bound the powers of darkness. When we got there, the man was very nice to us. He listened as we presented Christ to him, and he believed and accepted Christ as his Saviour. Praise God! Is anything too hard for God? No! No! No! A thousand times no!

Another time, I was in Kentucky where some people gave me the names of some bootleggers. You know what bootleggers are. They sell illegal whiskey, and they are tough characters in Kentucky. They asked me if I would go and witness to these men. We went, but before we left, we stood on Matthew 18:19. We bound the power of Satan, and we claimed that God's power would work.

We went into one home, and they thought we had come to buy illegal whiskey. He asked, "What can I do for you?"

I said, "Sir, it's not what you can do for me, it's what Jesus can do for you."

The man was real nice to us. These kind of people are not usually nice to you if you come to talk to them about the Lord. But, when you realize the power you have in Christ, you will see amazing changes take place.

There were three people sitting at a table, and he invited us to sit down. I began to talk to them and share with them what God had done in my life. The miracles that had taken place in my life. How God had saved me, and healed me. I told them how God caused me to grow when I was twenty-six years old from 4'9½" to 6'1".

I told them Jesus hadn't changed and what He did two thousand years ago, He'll do today. The man said, "Do you think Jesus would save me?"

I said, "No, I don't think so. I know so. The Bible tells us that if we believe in our hearts and confess with our mouths, we shall be saved. Whosoever calls upon the name of the Lord shall be saved."

He just couldn't believe that God would save *him.* I asked him if he believed the Bible, which he did. We began to read the Bible. One man started telling me how mean he had been. He showed me the bullet wounds that were in his body from gunfights and knife fights. I tried to get away from this and back to talking about Jesus. (When witnessing, avoid getting off on other subjects. You are there to tell about Jesus.)

I kept talking about Jesus, and told him how much Jesus loved him. When we had been there about forty minutes, I saw God touch one of the men across from me. A tear came streaking out of his eye. I went to where he sat and asked him if he would like to pray and ask the Lord to come into his heart. He said, "Yes, I would."

That man prayed and invited Jesus into his heart. That day we saw three hardhearted bootleggers saved for the glory of Jesus. Everybody else who had talked to them had been thrown out, but we had bound the power of Satan. Is anything too hard for God? No! All we have to do is have faith that God's power will work.

He says, "Go ye into all the world." That means the world around your home. It means your next-door neighbor, your friends, your family, and anyone else you come in contact with. The Lord will provide clear-cut openings if you are available to Him. And He will give you the strength and the courage. In Christ, we are always victorious!

Love

"As the Father hath loved me, so have I loved you: continue ye in my love. If ye keep my commandments, ye shall abide in my love; even as I have kept my Father's commandments, and abide in his love. These things have I spoken unto you, that my joy might remain in you, and that your joy might be full. This is my commandment, That ye love one another, as I have loved you," John 15:9-12.

The Bible tells us "Love suffereth long, and is kind; love envieth not; love vaunteth not itself, is not puffed up, doth not behave itself unseemly, seeketh not her own, is not easily provoked, thinketh no evil" (I Cor. 13:4-5).

In the third verse of the same chapter we read, "Though I bestow all my goods to feed the poor, and though I give my body to be burned, and have not love, it profiteth me nothing." We see that no matter who we are, what we do, how much power we have, or how many gifts are operating in our lives, unless we have love, we are as sounding brass and a tinkling cymbal. We are to follow after love. We should also desire spiritual gifts, but unless we have love with them, they are useless. We need God's love in our hearts. Human love falls short, and in ourselves, we cannot love like we should.

I remember a time in my life when I didn't have the love I ought to have. It's not so easy to love people, sometimes. Can we love the unlovely? Can we put our arm around that drunkard and tell him that we love him, even when he is drunk? Women, can you put your arms around that prostitute and tell her you love her, and that Jesus loves her? Love is the key. God is love. God so loved the world. . .

The Lord began to do a work in me concerning love. Oh, I loved others, and could go from door-to-door witnessing, and I had enough love for some things. But there were just some people I was not capable of loving. I didn't hate them, but I didn't have the love for them that I needed. Some of these people were the hippies.

I was in the gift shop business at Riceville, Tennessee, on Highway 11, and these hippies would come in in droves. They would come in with one thing in mind, and that was to steal. I got the opinion they were no good, and I would even call them "the no-good, sorry, stinking bums." That was the way I felt about them. These people stole me blind. I lost a lot of money each year because a full carload of them would come in, and you couldn't watch all of them.

I was a Christian, and I loved God, and I was witnessing and winning people to Christ, but I just couldn't love those people.

After I received the baptism of the Holy Spirit, the Lord began to purge me. One day when I was going down the road, the Lord spoke to me, "Jimmy, do you see that hitchhiker?"

I said, "Yes, Lord."

He said, "Pick him up!"

I said, "God, you must be kidding! You know, God, that I can't do that."

The minute the Lord told me to do that, the devil

said that I had better not. He told me the guy would kill me, would steal my money, and would steal my car. All of these bad thoughts and negative thoughts would come into my mind.

But the Lord said, "Jimmy, does not my Word say, 'Greater is he that is in you than he that is in the world?' " God reminded me that I didn't have to be afraid, that perfect love casts out *all* fear. He reminded me that He was not a man that He should lie. He told me I needed confidence in His Word and rebuke the devil. He told me to rebuke the bad thoughts, and they would flee from me.

Then He began to deal with me on love. I told the Lord, "Lord, I just don't have the love that I ought to have for these people. Lord, I am not capable of having the love to love them because they have stolen so much from me for years." Then I said, "Lord, will you please give me this love that I can love them. If you will put that love in my heart for them, I will gladly pick them up and witness to them."

Two or three weeks later as I was going down the road, I saw some hippies on the side of the road. The Lord said, "Jimmy, I want you to pick up these people and tell them about me."

I still didn't have that love, and I said, "Lord, I can't do that." The Lord reminded me, though, that the Bible says that we can do all things through Christ who strengthens us. We can't do it in ourselves, but through Christ. God was taking the chaff out of me, and the impurities.

We need to have the mind of Christ. We need the renewing of our minds (Eph. 4:23). The Lord began to do this for me.

As I was going down the road again one day, I saw a hippie. The same bad thoughts came into my mind. The same bad feelings that Jimmy Maynor had for them came to the surface. The Lord said, "Jimmy, I love that hippie,

69

just as much as I love you. I died for him just as much as I died for you, and I don't want you to ever forget that. Remember, that boy is some mother's son, and she cares for him, and I care for him."

Sometimes, we try to get out of things by putting out fleeces. That's what I did. I said, "Lord, if that is really you speaking to me, and if you really want me to pick up a hippie and tell him about Jesus, I'm going to Benton, about thirteen miles from here. Right there in Benton is a bridge, and if you will have one standing on that bridge, (Not two, Lord. Just one!) I'll pick him up and tell him about Jesus."

The Bible doesn't say that those who are led by fleeces are the sons of God. And if you keep on going by fleeces, you are going to wind up getting fleeced spiritually. I knew not to operate or depend on fleeces, because those that are led by the Spirit of God, they are the sons of God. But God is so good and bears with us and our foolish ways, sometimes.

As I got to this bridge, there stood a hippie, right on the bridge where I asked God to have him standing. This was the worst-looking hippie I had ever seen in my life. He was dirty. He was filthy. This man was just unbelievable! Long hair, a beard, and he had been in a fight. He was bleeding some, but I promised God that I would pick him up and witness to him, so I pulled over in my Oldsmobile and invited him to get in and ride.

He was going to Chattanooga. As we were going down the road, I began to tell him what Jesus meant to me. That is the greatest witness you have—what Jesus means to you. People can't argue with the experience you have had with the Lord. I told him what Jesus had done for me. How I had been away from God, and God had done so much for me. He had let me live when I was dying, had healed me, and put my feet upon a solid rock. But it seemed that this man was not impressed at all with what I was saying. He had been on drugs, alcohol, you name it, he had been there. But as we went down the road, I kept telling him about Jesus. You have a captive audience when you pick up hitchhikers, because they can't go anywhere. They have to sit there and listen to you.

We got to Cleveland, Tennessee, and the Lord quickened a Scripture to me: Matthew 18:18-19, the Scripture on binding and loosing. I had a friend in Cleveland who worked in a Christian bookstore. I stopped there and had a sister agree with me. We held hands with this man. His name was James. I said, "Devil! I bind your power in Jesus' name, according to God's Word. It gives me the power to bind and loose, so I bind your power in Jesus' name, and I claim salvation for James. Father, I thank you for saving him. Now, Lord, I ask you to deal with him and bring him into the kingdom of God."

We went on our way. I put him on the bus for Chattanooga, and the Lord told me to give him $20. I couldn't believe that God would want me to give him any money. After all, you just don't give drug addicts and alcoholics $20 bills. But I had the impression from the Lord to do it. I knew there was no use arguing about it, because the Lord always wins. So I gave him the money.

I have argued with the Lord sometimes, but He always wins. It wasn't exactly that I didn't want to give the man the money, but I thought he would probably buy dope with it. I just couldn't understand the working of the Lord. And sometimes we don't, but we just need to obey. Obedience is better than sacrifice.

After I put him on the bus, I began to say, "Thank you, Lord, for saving James. Thank you, Lord, for saving James."

The Bible says that we can have what we say, if we believe and do not doubt (Mark 11:23). "Thank you,

71

Lord, for saving James, and, devil, you cannot have this man. Your power is broken, and I claim this man for the Kingdom of God. Thank you, Lord, for saving James."

I sounded like a broken record, I said it so much. I said it because I had learned a lesson that when you boldly confess, then and only then, do you possess. You have to believe in your heart and confess with your mouth anything you want from God. If it is the salvation of a loved one, or a healing, or whatever, you have to believe it and confess it with your mouth.

I kept confessing, "Thank you, Lord, for saving James. My sister in Christ and I have claimed that the devil's power would be broken over this man and that he would be saved." Several times a day I would say this. When you do this regarding claiming a lost loved one, you stand in faith, nothing wavering. "But let him ask in faith, nothing wavering. For he that wavereth is like a wave of the sea driven with the wind and tossed. For let not that man think that he shall receive any thing of the Lord" (James 1:6-7). I didn't doubt and waver regarding James, and after about a week, I received a letter from him.

He had gotten to Chattanooga, and just like I thought, he took the money I had given him and got drunk. Then he got on drugs. I think he mixed the drugs and alcohol. I don't know the exact story. But he ended up getting sick and had to go to the hospital. When he got to the hospital, he thought he was dying. He remembered what I had said about Jesus and salvation. He got the little Bible out that I had given him and got on his knees beside the bed and asked the Lord Jesus to come into his heart, forgive him of his sins, and save his soul. And, praise God, Jesus saved him!

This was a new experience for me. I had not had the love for that man like I should have had when I picked him up, but I asked God to give me the love and help me

72

to love him, and He did! I began to pick up hippies and all kinds of hitchhikers, and I had a love for them that I never had before. It just delights me now to pick them up and tell them about Jesus. Since that day, I have picked up many people and led them to Christ in my car.

God wants us to have the love that will flow forth from us to others no matter what they look like, no matter what they act like. Let us prove our love by our actions. James 1:22-25 says, "But be ye doers of the word, and not hearers only, deceiving your own selves. For if any be a hearer of the word, and not a doer, he is like unto a man beholding his natural face in a glass: for he beholdeth himself, and goeth his way, and straightway forgetteth what manner of man he was. But whoso looketh into the perfect law of liberty, and continueth therein, he being not a forgetful hearer, but a doer of the word, this man shall be blessed in his deed" (James 1:22-25). We need to be doers and have love one for another.

My friend Dale Smith, and I were going home from Riceville, Tennessee, on Highway 11. It was one of those cold and rainy nights. My car lights picked up a colored man walking up the road. It was about midnight, and it looked like he had just about taken all he could take from the way he walked. I felt sorry for the man and asked the Lord to please help him. The Lord told me that I was His disciple and that I was in a position to help him.

We took him to Dale's house and gave him something to eat. We told him about Jesus, and told him that Jesus would forgive him of his sins and give him a new life. The man was saved and filled with the Spirit. He spent the night with Dale. Before he was put on a bus the next morning, he told Dale that he had planned to go to Asheville, North Carolina, to get even with a man who had wronged him. He said he might even have killed the man. He was also going to meet four other men and rob some service stations they had under surveillance. But, praise God, since he had met Jesus, he had no desire to do those things. Now God has called him to preach the Gospel and he is presently studying to be an army chaplain.

We never know what God will do through us, and we never know what He will do through those we touch for Him. Sometimes it's the most unlikely ones from a natural standpoint that He uses the most. We are prone to look on the outward appearance, but God looks at the heart.

"My brethren, have not the faith of our Lord Jesus Christ, the Lord of glory, with respect of persons. For if there come unto your assembly a man with a gold ring, in goodly apparel, and there come in also a poor man in vile raiment; and ye have respect to him that weareth the gay clothing, and say unto him, Sit thou here in a good place; and say to the poor, Stand thou there, or sit here under my footstool: are ye not then partial in yourselves, and are become judges of evil thoughts? Hearken, my beloved brethren, Hath not God chosen the poor of this world rich in faith, and heirs of the kingdom which he hath promised to them that love him? But ye have despised the poor. Do not rich men oppress you, and draw you before the judgment seats? Do not they blaspheme that worthy name by the which ye are called? If ye fulfil the royal law according to the scripture, Thou shalt love thy neighbour as thyself, as ye do well: But if ye have respect to persons, ye commit sin, and are convinced of the law as transgressors" (James 2:1-9).

Let's ask God to instill His love in our hearts that we might love all people and go out in the Name of Jesus without respect of persons. The Word of God, administered in love, is what will change people and change the world.

The Vision

"And the devil that deceived them was cast into the lake of fire and brimstone, where the beast and the false prophet are, and shall be tormented day and night for ever and ever" (Rev. 20:10).

In January 1974 I was with Norvel Hayes at the Indianapolis Regional Convention of the Full Gospel Business Men's Fellowship. After the convention was over, we went to a church nearby to hold some meetings. One night while Norvel was speaking, I had a burden come on me. I felt that if I didn't pray, I was going to die. I just had to pray, but I didn't want to disturb the meeting. In a few minutes, Norvel said, "If there is anyone who feels the need to pray, come on up to the altar and pray." I got up out of my seat, went to the altar, knelt down, and began to pray in the Spirit.

After praying a while, God took me in the Spirit, and I was out of this natural world. I saw a lake of fire that is partly described in Revelation 20:10. It was a huge lake of fire. There were very high cliffs all around it. From the top of these cliffs down to the fire was a long, long way. The cliffs were impassable, so that those who were in this place could in no way get out. The liquid in this lake was like volcanic lava. There were flames leaping up. I have no words to describe this place.

I saw the road that led there. On this road were all kinds of people. A great multitude! I saw them walking, seemingly unconcerned. It was as if they did not know where they were going. As they walked down this road, it came to an end at the edge of the lake of fire, and they dropped off a cliff into the lake. As they saw the burning hell, they seemed for the first time to realize where they were going. I looked upon their faces. I saw the frightened looks. Then they dropped into the chasm below.

Words cannot describe the screams I heard. Many of these people never did believe there was a burning hell. Many of them meant to give their lives to God some time, but never did. And I felt in the Spirit, that a large number of these people were people who thought they were going to Heaven, but they had been deceived because they did not know the Word. They had put their faith in what their denomination taught them instead of knowing the Word of God. We should know the Bible well enough to tell if someone is teaching something that is not backed up by the Bible.

As I saw these people drop into the lake of fire, I realized that what I was seeing was something that was going to happen in the future. I cried out to the Lord, *"Lord, have mercy on these people!"*

He said, "You go and warn people to turn from their sins and believe in Me while there is yet time. The fields are white, but the laborers are few."

We need to warn people while there is yet time. We need to be soul-winners. We need to witness daily. Some of our best Bible scholars are not soul-winners. Some of our best pastors are not witnessing like they should. I have known many pastors who are not leading very many people to Christ.

God has commissioned us to go forth. God is raising

up a great army in these last days. This army will be mainly an army of youth, because the young people are getting on fire for God. The adults don't come to witnessing and soul-winning seminars like they should. It's mostly the young people who are interested in doing something for Jesus. They are really getting "turned on." They are forming an army to go and tell the world about Jesus.

If this world is going to be won to Christ, it is through people who get a vision of the world going to hell, and who go forth and proclaim the Good News of the Lord Jesus Christ. If the world is going to be won to Christ in our lifetime, then everyone must do his part. The preachers, the evangelists alone, cannot do it. They are failing, failing, failing! The church of today is failing to do what she is supposed to do. She is not reaching the lost. I know there are exceptions, and we could point to some who are. But as a whole, they are not.

Too many people are getting their eyes on miracles. Praise God for miracles! They are getting their eyes on healing, and praise God for healing! Most charismatic churches, most Full Gospel churches are missing the mark. I see signs that read: "Full Gospel Church," unless it is a witnessing church and going out and winning the lost, they should take their sign down, because they are not a Full Gospel Church. To be a Full Gospel Church, we have to be a witnessing church and stress salvation, as well as healings and miracles.

You can have the most powerful radio station in the world. You can have the best radio that money can buy, but until you get tuned in to the right frequency, my friend, you are not going to pick up what's coming across the airwaves. We need to get tuned in to the Spirit and know what the Spirit is saying.

God wants to raise up a great army who will go in the Name of Jesus and conquer the enemy, kick the devil in the teeth, so to speak, and win the lost world for Christ. This is happening in other countries all around the world. But here in the United States we are failing.

Purpose in your heart today to join this great army. Say, *Lord, here I am! Take me and use me. Lord, here I am! Help me to be a soul-winner. Help me to be a witness. Help me to be what you would have me to be.*

You might say you don't know how, and that you're too weak. But, my friend, God will show you how, and He will give you strength. If you will begin each day with, "Lord, I am available," the Lord will begin to do a work in your life. He'll do a deep work, and He will teach you how to be successful in witnessing.

Remember, Satan is a murderer and a liar. He wants to rob us of our joy in our spiritual life. He wants to rob us of our sharing the Gospel. He wants to rob people of their salvation. He is our enemy and keeps us from being good soldiers by getting us entangled with affairs of this life. He'll try to weaken us and hinder us from witnessing, by robbing us of time to study the Bible and pray.

How much time do we give Jesus to be available to witness? How do we spend the biggest part of our time? How much time do we devote to recreation, hobbies, friends, TV, Bible study, church witnessing? We should be spending the greatest part of our free time for the Lord.

I know we have to work to make a living. But we need to work for the Lord while it is yet day. The night cometh, when no man can work. Surely, we can give two or three hours a week of our time to witness. Go from house-to-house like they did in the early church! They ceased not to preach and teach Christ Jesus, house-to-house. That's the way they did it, and it was effective.

I find that out of ten people that I visit, if I can get inside their homes, five of them will get saved. The world is starving for love. The world is starving for people to

78

come and tell them about Jesus. The Bible says, "Believe on the Lord Jesus Christ, and ye shall be saved." Many people do not know how to believe on the Lord Jesus Christ. To many of us, believing was easy, but to countless thousands, the words "believe" and "faith" are mysterious and hard to understand. They say they have always believed in the Bible, but they don't know whether or not they are saved. Salvation is a gift of God, and they believe this, but they have never reached out and received it.

The devil has "blinded the minds of them which believe not, lest the light of the glorious Gospel of Christ, who is the image of God, should shine unto them" (II Cor. 4:4). We need to show them from the Word how they can accept God's gift of eternal life. When you witness for Christ, it is God who is at work in you by the power of the Holy Spirit. You give forth God's message that Christ died for our sins, was buried and was raised on the third day according to the Scripture, and that through His Name, everyone who believes in Him has received forgiveness of sin. As you obey the Lord, you shall go and bear fruit, for He is able to do exceeding abundantly above all that we ask or think, according to the power that works within us.

Begin witnessing like Andrew, who found his own brother, Simon, and brought him to Jesus. Go obediently like Philip, whom God told to arise and go, and he obeyed and went. He met an unsaved man from Ethiopia and preached Jesus to him.

"And this Gospel of the Kingdom shall be preached in all the world for a witness to all nations" (Matt. 24:14). We have been given an assignment. Let's do our part in spreading the Gospel in all the world. Let's get a vision of what Jesus came to save us from! Let's get a vision of what is ahead for the lost man, woman, boy, or girl! You might

79

not have a vision like I had, but the Bible describes the horrors of hell. Let's warn and rescue as many as we can by God's grace and help!

Standing in the Gap
for the Lost

"Therefore, I say unto you, what things soever ye desire, when ye pray, believe that ye receive them, and ye shall have them" (Mark 11:24).

Most of us have lost brothers, lost sisters, lost husbands, lost wives, lost friends, lost neighbors, lost children, or lost parents. We can stand in the gap for them and pray the prayer of faith, and they will be saved.

Faith is a wonderful thing. Faith will work anything, regardless of what it is. Most people will say, "I don't have much faith." The Bible tells us that every person has received a measure of faith. We find that in Romans 12:3. If we want to have more faith, we can, because Romans 10:17 says, "Faith cometh by hearing, and hearing by the word of God." If you want more faith, bury your face in the Bible. If you plant something dead, it won't grow. But the Word is living, and as it is implanted in your heart, faith will spring up and grow. Hebrews 11:6 tells us, "Without faith it is impossible to please him."

The first verse of chapter 11 of Hebrews tells us that "Faith is the substance of things hoped for, the evidence of things not seen." If we want anything from God, we can receive it through faith. Faith works for salvation. Faith works for healing. Faith works for claiming lost loved ones. If you have faith and do not waver, you can receive anything you need. "But let him ask in faith, nothing wavering. For he that wavereth is like a wave of the sea driven with the wind and tossed. For let not that man think he shall receive any thing of the Lord" (James 1:6-7). But if we ask in faith, we *will* receive.

There was a certain person I was very interested in seeing rededicate his life to God who had been in church most of his life. He got out of fellowship with God, and he quit going to church. Everybody in the community had been to talk to him. The pastor had pleaded with him. I had been to see him many times, but to no avail.

This was really heavy upon my heart. I decided I was going to lock myself in my home in fasting and prayer for this man until I heard from heaven. On the third day of fasting and prayer, I said, "But, Jesus, I've done this and I've done that. I've done this and I've done that. I've tried this and I've tried that."

And the Lord said, "Jimmy, that is just the trouble. You have been trying to do it, and other people have been trying to do it. You have not been trusting me, steadfast in the faith."

A scripture came to me, "Casting all your care upon him; for he careth for you" (I Pet. 5:7). The Lord spoke to me, and said, "Haven't I taught you in my Word to cast all your cares upon me, for I care for you? The reason this person has not been brought into the Kingdom is because people have been trying to do it. As long as you worry about it, as long as you are upset about it, you haven't given it to me and are not holding steadfast in faith."

That day, I picked up this person, in my mind's eye, and I just threw him upon the Lord. I had been carrying this burden around for three years.

"For verily I say unto you, that whosoever shall say

unto this mountain, Be thou removed, and be thou cast into the sea; and shall not doubt in his heart, but shall believe that those things which he saith shall come to pass; he shall have whatsoever he saith" (Mark 11:23). This scripture says we can have whatsoever we say if we believe and do not doubt. I cast this man upon the Lord. I stood on the Word, and I said, "Devil! I break your power over this man in the Name of Jesus, and I *command you* (I'm not asking you) to take your hands off this man, for I claim him in the Name of Jesus. Devil, I tell you right now you cannot have this man. I claim his soul for the kingdom of God."

The Bible says you have to be steadfast and not waver. I said this every day. Sometimes I would say it six or seven times a day. I would say it out loud. It's hard to *say* something, unless you say it out loud.

It wasn't long afterward that I was talking with a lady who said she was so concerned about this man. I said, "Well, I'm not concerned about him at all, because he is getting ready to come into the kingdom of God!"

She said, "He is?"

I said, "That's right. He is, because I prayed the prayer of faith and am standing steadfast, and God will bring him in."

I did this for three weeks. You would have to know this situation to appreciate it. For three years, no one could touch this person. No one could witness to him. But when I stood steadfast, unwavering, and believing, God began to do a work in him. He got up one morning, and he said he just had the notion to go to church. Praise God! He went to church, and on the second song, he got under conviction, and he ran to the altar and made things right between he and the Lord. Praise God! This shows the power of God. It is not limited.

I have done this many times. There was a man in our

83

community who didn't know the Lord. This man was past talking to, too. You could go and visit him, and he wouldn't even talk to you. I said, "I'm just going to turn my faith loose on him."

I went to this elderly man, looked him in the eye and said, "Sir, I am claiming your life for the kingdom of God. I have broken the power of Satan over you, and you are going to be saved." I know this sounds a little crazy, but that's exactly what I did.

With his permission, I laid my hands on this man and claimed him for God. I did exactly the same as before. I began to praise God for the salvation of his soul. I got up each morning, saying, "Thank you, God, for saving him! Thank you, God, for saving him. Devil, you can't have him! My faith will bring the power of God to him!"

I was out on the road ministering and was gone four weeks. When I came back, a man came to me and said, "Guess what happened at church Sunday?"

I said, "Well, I don't know."

He said, "You know this certain man came to church, and when the invitation was given, he walked the aisle and received Christ as his Saviour." Praise God forevermore! That's the power of God!

If you have loved ones, you can claim their souls for the Kingdom of God. Your faith, not anything else, can bring God's power to them to shake them to their very foundation. Whatever it takes, God's power can perform it and do it. You just have to believe it and stand on the Word of God. Give them to God! As long as you are worrying about it, as long as you are nervous about the situation, you are not trusting God. When you trust God, and you cast that care upon Him, *you* won't be carrying the burden anymore. If anybody comes to you and says, "Well, what about Uncle Joe?", just say, "Don't worry about Uncle Joe, because he is coming in. Praise God! I prayed the prayer of faith for him." Be steadfast and un-wavering! Confess it, and you'll possess it!

One night in a service where I had taught about standing in the gap, I had people come forward who want-ed to do this for some loved one. I would ask them the first name and pray the prayer of faith with them. There was a woman there who I agreed with for the salvation of her two sons. Before she got back home, both of them were saved. They had been watching the Billy Graham Crusade on TV and got under conviction and were saved.

When a friend of mine, Norvel Hayes, who has a full-time Christian ministry, was in a church in Florida, he was teaching and bringing a message on "Standing in the Gap for your Children." This was for parents whose children were in trouble, or who were on drugs, etc. He told them if they would stand in the gap, by faith, God would bring them in.

There was a woman there whose daughter just left one day, and she hadn't heard from her in a very long time. She got up and challenged Norvel and said, "You mean to tell me that God will tell me where my child is?"

Norvel said, "Absolutely! If you will pray the prayer of faith, and believe it, God will show you."

So they prayed and agreed that God was going to show her where her daughter was, and that He would have her call home. Norvel warned her, pointing his finger at her, "You'd better not waver now."

After several weeks of standing in the gap for her child, the devil began to come at her and tell her that she was dead and that there was no use in her standing in the gap for her daughter. She said she had just about given up hope, but she could see Norvel Hayes pointing his finger at her and saying, "You had better not waver, woman. I warn you, you had better not waver."

She said she suddenly just felt the power of God come into her, and she said, "No, no! Devil, get away from me. I am not going to waver."

In a few days she picked up the telephone when it rang, and on the other end was the voice of her daughter, and she said, "Mama, mama, I am tired of living in sin. Will you and daddy come and get me?"

Of course, they were joyful and praising God. They got into their car and drove to another state where their daughter had been living and picked her up. When she got into the car, she was crying. With tears streaming down her face, she said, "Mama, I'm tired of this life. Just the other day, I began to think about what a good life I used to have with you and daddy. I'm tired of living in sin. I want to get saved."

They took her back home, and soon she received Christ as her Saviour. You see what the power of God can do when you stand steadfast for your loved ones. God's power will simply go to them, convict them of sin, and bring them to the knowledge of His son, Jesus.

"And I sought for a man among them, that he should make up the hedge, and stand in the gap before me for the land, that I should not destroy it: but I found none" (Ezek. 22:30).

The Lord's heart is yearning for our loved ones to come to Him. His Father-heart is aching for his prodigal sons. Will we stand in the gap for them? It might take a few days, or it might take a few weeks. It might take a few months, or even a few years. But it *will* come to pass!

Dealing with those
Who Have Difficulties

In meeting problems, we must depend on the Word of God for a solution. People have many different reasons for not becoming Christians, and we should be prepared with answers from the Bible.

The Bible needs no defense, and we do not need to argue. Just relax and listen to what the person says. Then, at the first opportunity, tell them what Christ means to you. As soon as your host realizes that you have not come to argue or cram Jesus down his throat, but that you love Jesus and just want him to know it, chances are he will relax and become more hospitable.

"But foolish and unlearned questions avoid, knowing that they do gender strifes. And the servant of the Lord must not strive; but be gentle unto all men, apt to teach, patient, in meekness instructing those that oppose themselves; if God peradventure will give them repentance to the acknowledging of the truth" (II Tim. 2:23, 25).

We must, under no circumstances, be drawn into an argument as nothing can be gained by it. You will find it is very difficult to win an argument and a soul at the same time. Some unsaved men will try to draw you into a sharp discussion so that they can show off their knowledge of science, or evolution, or some other subject. Avoid such useless discussions as your purpose is not to reason with men concerning personal opinions, but to convey to them the message from God's Word.

As a messenger, it is not your place to argue with men about the message. It is your duty to deliver it to them. It never pays to be overcome by any situation, no matter how difficult.

If the person with whom you are conversing seems rather harsh, discourteous, or ill-mannered, no better method or answer could possibly work than that of remaining master of the situation by your gentle, loving spirit. "A soft answer turneth away wrath: but grievous words stir up anger" (Prov. 15:1). Since we are utterly dependent upon the Holy Spirit when we witness, we must remain gentle and humble. The Holy Spirit cannot work where there is strife.

EXCUSES AND SCRIPTURAL ANSWERS:
THE UNCONCERNED—Use Scriptures that will bring conviction of sin:

- *John 3:18,* "He that believeth on him is not condemned: but he that believeth not is condemned already, because he hath not believed in the name of the only begotten son of God."
- *Romans 6:23,* "For the wages of sin is death; but the gift of God is eternal life through Jesus Christ, our Lord."
- *Luke 13:3,* "I tell you, Nay: but, except ye repent, ye shall all likewise perish."
- *Prov. 27:1,* "Boast not thyself of tomorrow; for thou knowest not what a day may bring forth."
- *Hebrews 2:3,* "How shall we escape, if we neglect so great salvation."

THE MORALIST—Use Scripture references on sin of

self-righteousness:

- *Isaiah 53:6,* "All we like sheep have gone astray; we have turned every one to his own way; and the Lord hath laid on him the iniquity of us all."
- *Isaiah 64:6,* "But we are all as an unclean thing, and all our righteousnesses are as filthy rags."
- *Titus 3:5,* "Not by works of righteousness which we have done, but according to his mercy he saved us."
- *Romans 3:10,* "There is none righteous, no, not one."
- *Ephesians 2:8-9,* "For by grace are ye saved through faith; and that not of yourselves: it is the gift of God: not of works, lest any man should boast."

HYPOCRITES IN THE CHURCH—We must look to Christ, and not to men for salvation:

- *John 3:14-15,* "And as Moses lifted up the serpent in the wilderness, even so must the Son of Man be lifted up: that whosoever believeth in him should not perish, but have eternal life."
- *Acts 17:30-31,* "And the times of this ignorance God winked at; but now commandeth all men everywhere to repent: because he hath appointed a day, in the which he will judge the world in righteousness by that man whom he hath ordained."
- *Isaiah 45:22,* "Look unto me, and be ye saved, all the ends of the earth: for I am God, and there is none else."
- *Romans 14:12,* "So then every one of us shall give account of himself to God."

THEY HAVE CROSSED A DEADLINE—When people feel

this way and think they cannot be saved, show how God is long-suffering, and that His love is everlasting.

- *II Peter 3:9,* "The Lord is not slack concerning his promise, as some men count slackness; but is longsuffering to us-ward, not willing that any should perish, but that all should come to repentance."
- *Psalm 86:5,* "For thou, Lord, art good, and ready to forgive; and plenteous in mercy unto all them that call upon thee."
- *John 6:37,* ". . . him that cometh to me; I will in no wise cast out."
- *Revelation 22:17,* "And the Spirit and the bride say, Come. And let him that heareth say, Come. And let him that is athirst come. And whosoever will, let him take the water of life freely."
- *Hebrews 7:25,* "Wherefore he is able also to save them to the uttermost that come unto God by him, seeing he ever liveth to make intercession for them."
- *Isaiah 1:18,* "Come now, and let us reason together, saith the Lord; though your sins be as scarlet, they shall be as white as snow; though they be red like crimson, they shall be as wool."

I CANNOT HOLD OUT—Show that Christ does the holding. Explain that it is perfectly natural to feel like this since being alienated from God. But when we accept Christ, we will become a new creature in Christ. Old desires, old habits, hatred, selfishness will all pass away. In place of the spiritual death that has reigned in our spirit, we will receive the nature of God and new desires and power to live a victorious life.

- *II Cor. 5:17,* "Therefore if any man be in Christ, he is a new creature; old things are passed away;

90

behold, all things are become new."

- *I John 5:12,* "He that hath the Son hath life; and he that hath not the Son of God hath not life."
- *I John 4:4,* ". . . greater is he that is in you, than he that is in the world."
- *Jude 24,* "Now unto him that is able to keep you from falling, and to present you faultless before the presence of his glory with exceeding joy."
- *I Cor. 10:13,* "There hath no temptation taken you but such as is common to man: but God is faithful, who will not suffer you to be tempted above that ye are able; but will with the temptation also make a way to escape, that ye may be able to bear it."
- *II Cor. 12:9-10,* "And he said unto me, My grace is sufficient for thee: for my strength is made perfect in weakness. Most gladly therefore will I rather glory in my infirmities, that the power of Christ may rest upn me. Therefore I take pleasure in infirmities, in reproaches, in necessities, in persecutions, in distress for Christ's sake: for when I am weak, then am I strong."
- *John 10:27-28,* "My sheep hear my voice, and I know them, and they follow me: and I give unto them eternal life; and they shall never perish, neither shall any man pluck them out of my hand. My Father, which gave them to me, is greater than all; and no man is able to pluck them out of my Father's hand."

THE CHRISTIAN LIFE IS TOO HARD—Christianity is not a religion, not a set of creeds of doctrine, but a walk with God.

- *John 1:12,* "But as many as received him, to them gave he power to become the sons of God, even to them that believe on his name."

- *Matthew 11:29-30,* "Take my yoke upon you, and learn of me; for I am meek and lowly in heart: and ye shall find rest unto your souls. For my yoke is easy, and my burden is light."
- *Phil. 4:13,* "I can do all things through Christ which strengtheneth me."
- *II Tim. 1:12,* ". . . for I know whom I have believed, and am persuaded that he is able to keep that which I have committed unto him against that day."

I AM NOT A BAD PERSON—Salvation is not based on being good or bad.

- *I John 1:8,* "If we say that we have no sin, we deceive ourselves, and the truth is not in us."
- *Eccles. 7:20,* "For there is not a just man upon earth, that doeth good, and sinneth not."
- *John 14:6,* "Jesus saith unto him, I am the way, the truth, and the life; no man cometh unto the Father, but by me."
- *Prov. 14:12,* "There is a way which seemeth right unto a man, but the end thereof are the ways of death."
- *John 3:3,* "Jesus answered and said unto him, Verily, verily, I say unto thee, Except a man be born again, he cannot see the kingdom of God."

I HAVE PLENTY OF TIME—The perils and the risk of delay.

- *II Cor. 6:2,* "For he saith, I have heard thee in a time accepted, and in the day of salvation have I succoured thee: behold, now is the accepted time; behold, now is the day of salvation."
- *John 3:18,* "He that believeth on him is not

condemned: but he that believeth not is condemned already, because he hath not believed in the name of the only begotten Son of God."

- *John 3:36,* "He that believeth on the Son hath everlasting life: and he that believeth not the Son shall not see life; but the wrath of God abideth on him."
- *Prov. 29:1,* "He, that being often reproved hardeneth his neck, shall suddenly be destroyed, and that without remedy."
- *James 4:13-14,* "Go to now, ye that say, Today or tomorrow we will go into such a city, and continue there a year, and buy and sell, and get gain: whereas ye know not what shall be on the morrow. For what is your life? It is even a vapour, that appeareth for a little time, and then vanisheth away."
- *Isaiah 55:6,* "Seek ye the Lord while he may be found, call ye upon him while he is near."

OTHER SCRIPTURE VERSES YOU SHOULD KNOW:

Psalms 9:17: The wicked shall be turned into hell, and all the nations that forget God.

Ezekiel 36:26: A new heart also will I give you, and a new spirit will I put within you: and I will take away the stony heart out of your flesh, and I will give you an heart of flesh.

Matthew 10:32: Whosoever shall confess me before men, him will I confess also before my Father which is in heaven.

Matthew 16:26: For what is a man profited, if he shall gain the whole world, and lose his own soul? or what shall a man give in exchange for his soul?

Luke 19:10: For the Son of man is come to seek and to save that which was lost.

Acts 4:12: Neither is there salvation in any other: for there is none other name under heaven given among men, whereby we must be saved.

Romans 14:11-12: For it is written, As I live, saith the Lord, every knee shall bow to me, and every tongue shall confess to God. So then everyone of us shall give account of himself to God.

II Corinthians 5:21: For he hath made him to be sin for us, who knew no sin; that we might be made the righteousness of God in him.

Hebrews 9:27: And as it is appointed unto men once to die, but after this the judgment.

II Timothy 3:16: All scripture is given by inspiration of God, and is profitable for doctrine, for reproof, for correction, for instruction in righteousness.

Overcoming Obstacles

There are many obstacles that you will have to learn to overcome in your witnessing. When you are out winning souls, the devil will do his utmost to try to disturb or confuse so your witness will be hindered.

TELEVISION. I find the best way when you are trying to witness to someone and the television is going full blast, is to ask the person, "Do you mind if I turn the TV down?"

Most of the time, they will get up and turn it off. Sometimes they won't turn it off, but they will turn it down, or tell you that you may turn it down. When I turn it down, I turn it way down. Not off, but low enough that I won't be disturbed. You might think that is rude, but remember souls are at stake.

CHILDREN. Many times the devil will use small children to hinder you in your witness. I have been witnessing many times to a mother, and the children would be playing. But the minute I said, "Jesus," they would start crying, screaming, and causing all kinds of disturbances.

This is one reason why you need someone with you when you go witnessing. Your prayer partner needs to be trained how to handle situations like this. He can take the child on his knee and play with them. Also, while he has them on his lap or knee, he needs to put his hand on them and silently plead the blood of Jesus and break the power of Satan. He should ask the Lord to quiet them down. While he is playing with the children, the person doing the witnessing can go on undisturbed. We must pray before we go and bind the power of Satan, and we should be prepared to handle disturbances such as these when they come up. You might not believe this, but I have even had small children kick me on the leg to get me to quit witnessing to their mother. If you go on the field and witness, you will find I am telling the truth.

HOUSE DOGS AND CATS. As a rule, cats are not bad about causing disturbances. House dogs are another matter. They can really be a problem. I believe most of them are demon possessed. As long as I talk about normal things, I have no trouble, but when I mention the name of Jesus, they start to act up. I have seen them jump in the person's lap to whom I was witnessing, and then growl at me. I have seen them go into a rage at the mention of the name of Jesus. I have had them bite me on the leg as I was trying to lead someone in prayer to accept Jesus as Saviour.

I have had people say, "My dog has never acted this way before. He sure does hate you. I don't know why he is like this."

I thought, "I do. The devil is in him."

Demons can and do live in animal bodies (Matthew 8:31-32). The job of your partner is to pick up the dog, or pet it, and silently bind the demons, pleading the blood of Jesus, and asking Jesus to help quiet down the dog or cat.

A RINGING TELEPHONE. The devil uses people to call while you are witnessing. I have had the phone ring as many as five or six times. The only thing you can do is to act as if nothing happened and go on witnessing again to the person when he gets off the telephone.

A FRIEND of the person you are witnessing to will sometimes come by while you are talking to your prospect. After being introduced, your prayer partner should pick up a conversation with his friend, so you can resume your witness. Don't try to witness to more than one person at a time if you can help it. We don't want to be rude in anyone's home, but you are there for one purpose and for one purpose only. That is, to lead that person to a saving knowledge of the Lord Jesus Christ. If they don't accept Jesus at that time, you are still sowing precious seed, for a harvest later on.

Preparation for the Home Visit

It will give you great confidence and make your home visit more successful, if you make certain preparations before going out.

First of all, there is the *INNER PREPARATION*. We must be cleansed from all known sin. 1st John 1:9 says, "If we confess our sins, he is faithful and just to forgive us our sins, and to cleanse us from all unrighteousness" (I John 1:9).

Go in a spirit of prayer. This is a must! If we spend much time in prayer, the devil will not be able to shoot us full of doubts and discouragement. Put on the whole armour of God, and above all things the shield of faith and the sword of the Spirit, which is the Word of God. Then you will be victorious.

Believe that God will do what He said He would do. Stand on His promises! Believe that the one in you is greater than he who is in the world. Know that you are under God's leadership and that you are fulfilling His command. Don't worry about feelings. Just remember, God is faithful! You can trust Him, and you are leaving the results to Him!

Also pray for the people you are going to visit. As an act of faith, thank God for what He is already doing to prepare the way for you. Place everything in His hands!

Secondly, there is the *OUTER PREPARATION.* We always want to be neat and clean, remembering that we are representing Christ. If you are going to be witnessing to a farmer, don't go dressed up in your best suit. Put on some casual clothes, or something more on his level. Paul said, "I am made all things to all men, that I might by all means save some" (I Cor. 9:22). If you are going to be witnessing in the slum areas, put on some blue jeans and just a regular shirt. You can win people to Christ better on their level.

TAKE A NEW TESTAMENT WITH YOU. Never carry a large Bible! If you have a small Bible and you can carry it in your purse or pocket, fine! Always keep your New Testament or Bible concealed until after you have been invited in and you are going to use it. If you come up to the door with a Bible under your arm, you might scare them off.

GO IN GROUPS OF TWO OR THREE. When I go witnessing, I like to have two other people with me. In most homes there are a couch and two chairs in the room. Before we knock on the door, we agree which one will do the witnessing. The other two will do the praying. As soon as we enter the room, the two who are going to pray, sit down in the chairs. That way the person that we came to witness to will sit on the couch beside the one who will do the talking. We want him to be able to see the Bible and to see what we are reading to him.

BE SMILING AND ALERT! As you walk up to the house, go happily, not boisterously. You will be able to tell if they have children if there are toys in the yard or on the porch. What kind of cars are parked in the yard? If there is a fishing boat, that tells you the man likes to fish. Anything you can find out about the person you are going to visit, will make your visit more meaningful and make it easier for you to carry on a conversation with him.

TALK ABOUT SUBJECTS IN WHICH THEY ARE INTERESTED. Jesus gave us an example of this. When he was dealing with farmers, He spoke about the sower. To the woman at the well, He spoke about water. We should, likewise, adapt our speech to the people with whom we are dealing.

Be sure you are courteous, kind, and compassionate. Most people know they are lost. We usually don't have to tell them that. They need someone to show love and concern about their destiny. If we don't have compassion for the lost, we won't be very effective. You might open the conversation by paying a compliment or referring to the pictures on the wall, flower arrangements, furniture, or especially the children, if there are any. Under the leadership of the Lord, you will quickly find out where their interests lie.

NEVER DO ALL THE TALKING. Let them know that you are interested in them and the things they have to say. Draw them out! Get them to talk about themselves and their interests.

For example, if I see a man has a boat in the yard, I might ask him, "Do you like to fish?"

He'll say, "Sure, I like to fish."

I'll ask him how fishing has been, and he might tell me of a big catch he has made recently. Perhaps I'll tell him that I am also interested in fishing, that I used to fish and enjoy fishing very much, but now the Lord has called me to be a fisher of men. Then after talking to him for a little while about something he enjoys talking about to break the ice, I just quietly ask him a question, "Do you know Jesus as your personal Saviour." Ask in love! Show a genuine concern! Never be pushy or forceful. *Never ask a person if he is a Christian.* Ninety percent of the people in the world claim to be Christians. Ask him if he knows

Christ as his personal Saviour.

There is an art in knowing *WHERE, HOW, WHEN,* and *WHAT* to say. We might possess a knowledge of the Word of God, but if we lack wisdom, our efforts will be of little or no influence or real benefit. We need the guidance and the sensitiveness of the Holy Spirit when dealing with people. Ask the Lord to help you in this area. Pray silently before you speak. And be gentle! The Holy Spirit is always gentle and tactful. Be a good representative!

NEVER HAVE A "HOLIER THAN THOU" ATTITUDE. Even with those who have gone into deep sin, we can truly say and feel, "Did not God have great love to send His Son into the world to die for sinners like you and me!" Remember, if it weren't for the grace of God, we would be in their shoes.

BE PATIENT AND PERSISTENT. You are dealing with a soul whose eternal destiny is at stake. "But that on the good ground are they, which in an honest and good heart, having heard the word, keep it, and bring forth fruit with patience" (Luke 8:15).

DO NOT GET DISCOURAGED. Be instant in season and out of season. Satan's number one tool is fear. His second tool is for people to get discouraged. Know that you are sowing the seed—the Word of God. It will bring forth fruit! God has said, "So shall my word be that goeth forth out of my mouth: it shall not return unto me void, but it shall accomplish that which I please, and it shall prosper in the thing whereto I sent it" (Isa. 55:11).

BE DIRECT AND STAY ON THE SUBJECT. The devil will try everything in the world to get you off the subject of witnessing. We have to control the conversation. Keep it focused around Christ. After the initial small-talk, don't get sidetracked onto other subjects. Have only one person do the witnessing. Many times I have seen people who could have been reached for Christ, but

101

because two or three people were trying to talk at the same time, the conversation would become confused and ineffective. The others should pray or take care of any problems that arise, such as, interruptions by dogs, cats, or children.

HAVE THE SALVATION VERSES UNDERLINED IN RED. This will catch the eye of the person you are witnessing to. If they are sitting next to you on the couch, they will be able to see the verses quickly and easily. It is important to not use too many scriptures, because you can only hold a person's attention for a certain amount of time. We should make our plan as direct and to the point as possible. The plan I use is very simple and effective. I use Romans 3:10, 3:23, 5:8, 10:9-10, and Revelation 3:20. You may use the scriptures that you desire, but this plan works for me. I have won many hundreds of people to Christ by presenting this plan.

THE DECISION. After showing him the plan of salvation, I simply extend my hand and say, "The Bible says that today is the day of salvation. It's not God's will that any should perish, but all should come to the knowledge of the truth. Now, John, just take my hand, and I will lead you in a prayer to accept Christ as your Saviour."

Never ask a "yes" or "no" question. If you ask a leading question like that, it gives him an opportunity to say no. Some might say this is a high-pressure method, but never mind! This is a spiritual warfare! While you have been talking to him, the Holy Spirit has been drawing him, but the devil will hinder as much as he can in every way he can. So be bold, and do everything you can to help him make a decision *FOR* Christ.

If the person gives you his hand, say immediately, "Let's bow our heads and pray."

SINNER'S PRAYER: Lead him in a sinner's prayer

to repent of his sins and accept Christ as Lord and Saviour of his life. Perhaps he wants to pray himself instead of being led by you. After the sinner's prayer, whether led by you or after he has prayed, pray a prayer of thanking the Lord for saving his soul.

You might say, "I know there are saints in Heaven rejoicing this minute. The Word tells us so. Thank you, Lord, for writing this person's name down in the Lamb's Book of Life. I thank you, Jesus, for saving him, because according to your Word, he is saved."

This kind of prayer will encourage him. Quote Revelation 3:20 to him, "Behold, I stand at the door and knock: if any man hear my voice, and open the door, I will come in to him and will sup with him, and he with me."

Say, "Did you ask him to come in?"

When the person says, "Yes, I did," tell him that since he asked Him to come in, He really did.

Ask him how he knows. They will usually say it is because the Bible says so. You will then be leaving them with a firm foundation on which to base their faith.

PUBLIC PROFESSION. Show them the importance of public profession. Quote Matthew 10:32-33, "Whosoever therefore shall confess me before men, him will I confess also before my Father which is in heaven. But whosoever shall deny me before men, him will I also deny before my Father which is in heaven." Also quote Romans 10:9 again, "That if thou shalt confess with thy mouth the Lord Jesus, and shalt believe in thine heart that God hath raised him from the dead, thou shalt be saved." If there is someone else in the house, have him tell them what has happened to him. Every time he confesses his salvation, it makes him stronger.

FELLOWSHIP. After the commitment, make a date to take the person to church. Continue to cultivate this young Christian. Lead him to follow Christ in baptism and join a local church fellowship. If you cannot come back for a follow-up, make a contact with someone in that community to do so. This is very important. Many times, I win people to Christ that I will probably never see again, and after arranging for someone else to do the follow-up, I remember to hold him up in prayer.

If you live close enough, continue to watch over the convert and lead him into a full knowledge of the Lord Jesus. Teach him who he is in Christ and the authority he has as a Son of God, and that he needs the power of the Holy Spirit in his life. Get to know him! You might invite him over to your home for a cook-out, or take him out to lunch. Follow-up work is a most important thing.

Always be radiant and full of joy. When you first approach your prospect and when doing follow-up, it's important to show qualities that would make him want what you have. It is easy for the person you are dealing with to detect whether or not you are earnest and sincere. No one enjoys meeting a grouch. The world is looking for a bright and cheerful countenance.

The personal worker must be a lover of souls. A genuine love is the greatest qualification to be a successful witness. We are going in Christ's stead. We are His ambassadors, and we must go with the attitude that we love them as though we had died for them. If we do not have this love, we may receive it by claiming it in Christ. "My God *SHALL* supply *ALL* your need," and this need of love is included in that promise (Phil 4:19).

We are the only contact Jesus has with a lost world. That is why we must love them as Christ loved them. It was this love that made Livingstone a successful missionary in the heart of Africa. Many whom he contacted had not been able to understand the language he had spoken, but long after he had passed from them, whenever his

104

name was mentioned, their faces shone with joy. They had not been able to understand his words, but they had understood the love that burned in his heart for them. Those with whom we come in contact, will respond to the love of Christ within our hearts for them.

A Typical Home Visit

Let's say I am going to witness to a man named John Brown. This will give you an idea of how you can put the information in this book into practical use. I am not telling you that you have to use this particular plan, because there are many good plans, but this one has worked for me in leading hundreds of people to the Lord.

I am taking Mary and Bill with me. We have prayed and bound the powers of Satan before going, claiming the promises of God. We have agreed that I will do the witnessing, and they will pray and take care of any disturbances, such as dogs, TV, children, etc.

As we go to the house, we notice if there is anything in the yard or driveway that will tell us something about the people, such a toys, bicycles, motorcycles, cars, or boats. When they come to the door, we are friendly and smiling, of course. I begin by telling them what church we are from, and that we came by to visit for a few minutes. (In most cases, I find they will invite you in if you are friendly.) If they say this is not a convenient time, just leave them a tract and tell them you will come back later. Always leave the door open so you will be welcome back later. Never press the issue or try to talk them into letting you come in.

If they invite you in, we go in immediately. Bill and Mary are quickly seated in the empty chairs, leaving the couch for John and I to sit on. This arrangement is best so John can see the Scriptures I am going to read to him. After being seated, I draw him into conversation and find out what he is interested in. We might talk about these things for a few minutes to break the ice and get acquainted.

Then I quickly say, "John, have you ever accepted Christ as your personal Saviour?"

If he says that he has not, then I tell him what Jesus did for me. I tell him about my life before I met Jesus, how I came to accept Jesus as my Saviour, and how my life has changed since. This part should not be over three minutes. As I end my testimony, I start presenting the plan of salvation. I simply pull out my Testament and say, "John, I want to show you a few Scripture verses."

Never ask the person if you can show him Scriptures, because this gives him a chance to say no. Just smoothly move into the reading of the Scriptures.

I begin by saying "John, do you believe the Bible is the Word of God?"

Most people will say yes. This gives me a good foundation. If a person says no, try to find out if he is serious. Some people say things they really do not mean, just trying to get rid of you. If you think he is really serious, then there is no use reading the Scriptures. Just relate some more about your personal experience, and get him to pray this prayer, "GOD, IF YOU ARE REALLY REAL, AND YOUR WORD IS REAL, I ASK YOU TO SHOW ME. I AM OPEN TO THE TRUTH. OPEN UP MY MIND AND MY HEART THAT I MAY KNOW THE TRUTH."

Leave him the plan of salvation and make plans to return at a later date. Remember, sometimes you are sowing seed.

If John says he believes the Bible is God's Word, then begin by reading to him Romans 3:10, "As it is written, there is none righteous, no, not one." Then I turn to Romans 3:23 and read, "For all have sinned, and come short of the glory of God."

I am reading this, but I hold the Bible where John can see what I am reading. I have underscored the verses in red so he can find them.

I then turn to Mary and say, "Mary, have you sinned and come short of the glory of God?"

She will say, "Yes, I have."

Then I turn to Bill and say, "Bill, have you sinned and come short of the glory of God?"

And he will say, "Yes, I have."

Then I say, "I have sinned and come short of the glory of God, too."

I am trying to get John to see that we are all sinners. Some of us are just saved by grace. I then ask John, "Have you sinned and come short of the glory of God?"

He in almost every case will say he is a sinner. This is very important. He needs to see and admit that he is a sinner. It is hard to reach a moral man for Christ who does not see his need.

Next I turn to Romans 5:8 and read, "But God commendeth his love toward us, in that, while we were yet sinners, Christ died for us." I show him that even though he is a sinner, Jesus loved him so much that He was willing to die for him, that through Him he might be saved. I also quote John 3:16.

Then I turn to Romans 6:23, "For the wages of sin is death; but the gift of God is eternal life through Jesus Christ our Lord." I show him we are not saved by good works, but by faith in God, and by receiving God's gift to man—salvation, Ephesians 2:8-9. It is very important to show him it is a gift. I sometimes use this illustration:

"John, if I came to your door, and it was your birthday and I brought you a gift because I loved you, what would you do?"

He would probably say he would accept it.

"John, Jesus did just that. He loved you so much that He has offered you the gift of salvation. All you have to do is accept it."

Then I turn to Romans 10:9-10 and read, "That if thou shalt confess with thy mouth the Lord Jesus, and shalt believe in thine heart that God hath raised from the dead, thou shalt be saved. For with the heart of man believeth unto righteousness: and with the mouth confession is made unto salvation."

I say, "John, there are two parts to being saved: God's part; and Man's part.

God has done his part. He loved you so much that He gave His son, Jesus, to die on the cross for your sins. If you will accept His gift of salvation and believe that Jesus is the Christ and that He died for your sins, ask Him to forgive you of your sins and turn from them, confessing Jesus as your Saviour, and ask Him to take control of your life, then you will be saved.

Then I turn to Rev. 3:20 and read, "Behold, I stand at the door and knock: if any man hear my voice, and open the door, I will come in to him, and will sup with him, and he with me."

"John, Jesus is knocking at your heart's door, and He wants to forgive you of all your sins and save you, giving you a home in heaven when you die. But for Him to do this, you must invite Him to come into your life."

I might use the following illustration: "John, if I came to your home, knocked, and asked you to let me in, it would be up to you decide to let me in or to not let me in. I would never come in where I was not welcome."

You might say, "Jimmy, I am busy now, and I don't

have time for you."

I would then leave very sad and disappointed. Later I might return and knock again, and say, "John, this is Jimmy. May I come in?"

Again you might tell me that you did not want me to come in, and again I would leave very sad and disappointed. But later I might come by and knock, hoping to be invited in. This time you might say, "Jimmy, come on in, " and you would open the door, and I would come in because I was welcome.

You might also say, "Jimmy, would you like a cup of coffee?"

And I would say, "Yes, I would."

Then we would sit down, sup coffee, talk to each other, and have fellowship with each other.

"John, Jesus is just like that. He is knocking at your heart's door, and He wants to come in and be your friend and fellowship with you. He wants to take away your fears and give you love, joy, peace, and the abundant life. He wants to come into your life, but you have to invite Him to come in. He will never force His way into your life. Jesus has been there knocking for a long time, wanting to come in and save you."

The Bible says today is the day of salvation. "For whosoever shall call upon the name of the Lord shall be saved," Romans 10:13. At this time, I just extend my hand, and say, "John, just take my hand, and I will lead you in a prayer to accept Jesus as your Saviour."

When John takes my hand, I lead him in a sinner's prayer to repent of his sins and accept Jesus as his Saviour, making it plain that he must really mean what he is saying and is serious. Then after leading him in the sinner's prayer, I tell John that now I want to pray. I pray, "Jesus, I thank you for saving John and for writing his name in the book of life. You said in your Word that if he would

110

invite you into his life, that you would come in. I know that you are there right now. Lord, take his life and mold it, and use him in your work. In Jesus name, I pray."

After rejoicing with him, I make a date to come back later and share with him about water baptism and church relationship. If I cannot come back because I am away from home, I make plans for someone else to do the follow-up work if at all possible.

THE STEPS WE TOOK TO BRING THIS PERSON TO JESUS

1. We began with a good foundation by finding out if he believed the Bible was the inspired Word of God.
2. We got him to see he was a sinner and needed to be saved. (Rom. 3:23)
3. We showed him we are not saved by good works, but by faith. That you could not be good enough to earn salvation. It is the gift of God. (Eph. 2:8-9; Rom. 6:23)
4. There are two parts to Salvation: God's part, and Man's part. God's part is that He gave His son, Jesus, to die on the cross for our sins, so that we could accept the gift of salvation and be saved. Man's part is to confess with his mouth the Lord Jesus, and believe in his heart that God raised Him from the dead. (Rom. 10:9-10)
5. The decision: To repent and turn away from his sins and invite Jesus to come into his life and take control, believing that Jesus is the Christ and confessing Him as His Saviour.

It is my prayer that this will help someone who has not known how to approach the lost person, or who has been at a loss for words to say.

Win Them by the Word

"So shall my word be that goeth forth out of my mouth: it shall not return unto me void, but it shall accomplish that which I please, and it shall prosper in the thing whereto I sent it" (Isa. 55:11).

For years I would tell people what Jesus meant to me, and this is effective to a certain degree. Once in a while I would get someone to come to church with me and hear the preached gospel. But I never was a very successful soul-winner until I began to win them by the Word.

"For the word of God is quick, and powerful, and sharper than any twoedged sword, piercing even to the dividing asunder of soul and spirit and of the joints and marrow, and is a discerner of the thoughts and intents of the heart" (Heb. 4:12).

The Word of God *IS* sharper than a twoedged sword. The Word of God *IS* quick and powerful, and it is the Word that convicts people of their sins. Until we take the Word and hold it forth to a lost and dying world, we will not see people brought into the kingdom of God.

It is absolutely necessary for the unsaved man to come in contact with the living Word of God. It is only by acting on it that a man can receive eternal life. He has to be made to realize his need of eternal life and how to

112

receive it. This information is found in the Word, and when it comes from the lips of someone who really believes it and has a loving interest in his personal salvation, it is very effective.

"That ye may be blameless and harmless, the sons of God, without rebuke, in the midst of a crooked and perverse nation, among whom ye shine as lights in the world; holding forth the word of life; that I may rejoice in the day of Christ, that I have not run in vain, neither labored in vain" (Phil. 2:15-16).

It's our privilege as Christians to offer this glorious message that promises joy, peace, and love, plus freedom from darkness and translation into God's marvelous light. We should hold it forth in an inviting and cheerful manner. It is not enough for us to have the word in our own lives and enjoy the reality of redemption ourselves. Jesus Christ wants to use us as channels through which He can send out this message of life and freedom to others.

People are waiting in bondage—waiting for the word that will set them free. The question is: How many Christians are doing this? Are you doing this?

A woman told me one time that she was letting her little light shine. That's fine! God wants us to let our light shine by our good lives. But until they hear and come in contact with the Word of God, they are not going to be saved. So very few unsaved people go to church, that it is up to every Christian, every disciple of Christ, to go forth and hold forth the word of God.

If we would only realize that people are not interested in religion, but something that will help them cope with their economic and social problems. The world is full of religion. Religion doesn't offer solutions to today's problems. If it did, there would be no need for my writing this book. We do not offer the unsaved a religion. *We offer them eternal life.* We offer them the nature of God. The

Gospel will make them new creatures in Christ Jesus.

We must walk in full fellowship with the Father so the person with whom we are dealing is conscious of the fact that we love him, and that Jesus loves him, and that we desire to help him. Never try to cram Jesus down anyone's throat. Just hold forth the Word of Life. If a man sees that you love him and are really interested in him, he will open up to you. This makes it easy for you to speak to him.

One time when I was in Chicago, Illinois, holding a seminar on soul-winning, I was given the name of a man that the church had been concerned about for a long time. For years, they had been trying to win him to Christ. He had been an alcoholic for something like 25-30 years. There is a right approach, and there is a wrong approach in soul-winning. They had been going to him with the wrong ones. They had been telling him that he must give up drinking. He must give up his cigarettes. He must give up cursing. You can never get a man to do these things before he is saved. God will meet a person at his point of need.

I went to see this man, and I just let him know that I cared, that the people of the church had been praying for him for many years, and that they cared, and I asked him one question. I said, "Sir, do you want to go to Heaven?"

He said, "Yes, of course, I do."

I said, "Let me show you what the Word of God says."

I simply took my Bible and read him five scriptures from the Word of God, showing him what he must do to be saved. One scripture I showed him was Romans 6:23, "The wages of sin is death; but the gift of God is eternal life through Jesus Christ our Lord." I shared with him that if I brought him a gift, he hadn't earned it, he hadn't bought it, but it was free because someone cared, because someone loved him and wanted to bring him a gift. I told him Jesus loved him, and that He would give him the gift of eternal life if he would only accept it by faith. I showed him what God had done for him, and in return, what he must do to be saved.

I shared with him Romans 10:9-10, "That if thou shalt confess with thy mouth the Lord Jesus, and shalt believe in thine heart that God hath raised him from the dead, thou shalt be saved. For with the heart man believeth unto righteousness; and with the mouth confession is made unto salvation."

I also shared with him Rev. 3:20, "Behold, I stand at the door and knock; if any man hear my voice and open the door, I will come in to him, and will sup with him and he with me." I told him Jesus was standing at his door, knocking.

This man asked me, "Do you think Jesus would save an old drunk like me?"

I said, "Yes, He will! It says here, if "any man" hear my voice and open the door, I will come in to him and sup with him and he with me."

"I'm not asking you to give up drinking and smoking. I am not asking you to quit doing the things you are doing. The only thing I am asking you to do this afternoon is to accept Jesus Christ as your Saviour. Then you will become a new creature in Christ Jesus. If you will follow the leading of the Spirit, the Spirit will help you to overcome the problem of being an alcoholic. He will help you to overcome the habit of cursing. The main thing you need is Jesus in your life. Would you like to kneel here with me and pray and invite Him to come into your heart?"

And the man said, "Yes, I would."

So we knelt together and prayed, and tears came from his eyes. He accepted Christ as his Saviour. Three days later he came to the church where I was teaching, and he made a public profession of faith.

You cannot always lead a man to Christ the first time you visit him. You will often have to make more than one visit. The secret of making your work effective is this: Each time you contact him, leave him a Scripture to think about. Human words and reasoning get no further than a man's intellect, but remember the Word of God reaches down into his very heart and really gets hold of him. The Word alone has the power to awaken a man from his spiritual stupor and cause him to turn to the Lord.

I have found that one or two Scriptures read and explained to a man have more power and more effect than many, many hours of reasoning and talking about religion. It is the Living Word that brings life. Jesus is the Living Word, and when the Holy Spirit quickens the Word to the heart, it brings salvation. Praise God!

"So shall my word be that goeth forth out of my mouth. It shall not return to me void, but it shall accomplish that which I please and it shall prosper in the thing whereto I sent it."

Visitation or Soul-Winning

"And how I kept back nothing that was profitable unto you, but have showed you, and have taught you publicly, and from house to house" (Acts 20:20).

It is very important for us to distinguish between a visitation program and soul-winning. They are two distinctly different things. The visitation program is centered on bringing people to church to be saved, whereas the soul-winning program is centered on going out and winning those who do not come to church.

The church has recovered part of the basic doctrines of early Christianity, but not since before the Dark Ages has personal soul-winning been her passion. There is evidence that the truth of personal evangelism is breaking out of its shell to come forth in full life and vigor before Christ returns. Everywhere alert preachers and dedicated Christians and lay people are talking about it. Writers are dealing with it. New programs are being started, but most approaches, thus far, have stopped short of what they should be.

Instead of having a soul-winning program, it has turned into a visitation program, more or less. Some people call it enlistment evangelism. There are many different versions, but most of them stop short of soul-winning.

117

Their programs are planned to get people to church to get them saved, but the Bible teaches that they went from house-to-house and door-to-door.

One form of enlistment evangelism is the bus ministry. There have been many thousands of people saved through bus ministries, and it is a great and marvelous thing. It is one of the greatest plans that the church is using today, but it is still geared to going out and getting people to come to church. There is nothing wrong with this. This is good, but that will account for only perhaps ten percent of the lost people. What about the other ninety percent? This form of evangelism is responsible for more conversions than anything else the church does in total evangelism, but it usually limits the results to those sinners who will come to church. What should we do about the others who will not come? We are going to have to get back to the early church's program of going out and winning souls from door-to-door.

Most churches today do not have a program at all for the ninety percent that won't come to church. Their usual concept is to go out and invite them. They tell them, "We have the most wonderful speaker in the world." They hire great speakers to come in, great revivalists and evangelists. They invite the sinners to come, which is good. Some will and do come. But we are never going to win the lost world to Christ by inviting people to come to church. We must go out where they are. We must meet them on their level.

If I could take ten people who are dedicated to witnessing for three hours per week it would be amazing how many souls would be saved in one year's time! I know this because I do it all the time. When I go to church to teach soul-winning and we go out during the afternoon and witness, we have seen marvelous results. In churches where they usually win about five people a year to Christ, after

118

three days of teaching soul-winning and with eight or ten people witnessing, we see thirty, forty, fifty, and sixty people saved in just a few days.

"How many people are going to get saved by knocking on doors and inviting them to come to church?" You will have much better results if you go to a house and instead of saying, "I'm from Valley Memorial Church. We'd like to invite you to come to our church," say, "We are visiting today from Valley Memorial Church. May we come in and talk to you for a few minutes?"

Most people will allow you to come in. You will find a few people say they are too busy, and that it's not convenient right then. Just leave courteously and come back at a later date.

One time I was witnessing, and a lady told me she didn't have time to visit. She was going to get her hair fixed, but told me I could come back later to see her. I waited about three days and went back. That time she said, "I'm sorry, I know I invited you to come back, but I'm cooking supper now. My husband will be home just any minute. I just don't have time."

She invited me to come back again, but she didn't expect me to do so. This is where you have to be persistent and determined. The third visit, she just gave up and invited me to come in.

Make return calls. It pays off! For those who do invite you in, sit down and witness to them about Jesus in love. Share the Scriptures with them. You will find a large percentage of these people will accept Christ as their Saviour. Where the people are is where you will win them.

It grieves my heart to go into churches and teach soul-winning where they have 150 people coming to Sunday school, but they are winning only fifteen, twenty, or thirty people a year to Christ. I know many, many laymen who win fifty, seventy-five or 100 souls a year. Just

119

one person! A salesman must be taught how to sell, and we must be taught how to witness. Training is so important!

Very few churches train their members in the art of soul-winning. You can scarcely find a Bible School or seminary where the curriculum includes courses to promote soul-winning. Yet, it is a glorious truth—the golden key to the success of the early church. With all the basic truths of the early church doctrine recovered today, it is time to discover what to do with all this truth. We must go out and share it with sinners. Once this truth regains its proper place in Christianity, writers will produce volumes of glorious and inspiring truths about soul-winning. Courses will be designed. Conferences will be held. Classes will be scheduled. Pastors will discover unlimited sources of fresh inspiration for teaching their congregation, both men and women, boys and girls, how to go out and witness and win souls like the early Christians did.

I believe before Jesus comes back, the Spirit will stir God's people into soul-winning action, and they will go out into the highways and witness to them. The Spirit will stir the hearts of people to not be content to sit inside their lovely buildings. They will not be content with their fine visitation programs. They will not be content to invite sinners to come to their meetings, but will come back to the pattern of the early church.

I do not discourage visitation. It has been a strong arm of church evangelism. Especially is this true when it includes a good bus ministry. We ought to get every sinner possible to come to church. They will then come under the hearing of the Word, which will convict them and bring them to repentance. But we are missing the mark, if we stop there. We ought to inaugurate plans and training courses and programs on personal evangelism, teaching

Christians how to actually lead a lost soul to Christ in his home. We ought to prove to the 90 percent of the world who are unchurched that we care about them.

Get outside of your church building! Witness on the highways! Witness on the byways! Witness in the barber shop! Witness in the grocery store and the super market! Witness at the service station, or wherever you come in contact with people. Then you, as Philip, and as the early church, will be a winner of souls, and not just a visitor.

Your Three-Minute Testimony

Not long ago, I heard Oral Roberts say on TV that if he had one hour to speak, he would have to do very little in the way of preparing his sermon. But on his telecast, he has only ten or eleven minutes. Therefore, he has to make every minute and every second count. This takes much preparation.

It is the same way with you and I when we are witnessing to someone who is in a hurry or is busy. Many times we have an opportunity to witness while a man is pumping gas into our tank, or at the barber shop, or while we are being checked out at the market. Unless we have perfected a way of getting our testimony across in a very short time, we will often miss a chance to witness. Many people would have two or three minutes to listen to us, so it is important for us to give a testimony that is short and to the point.

If you would take the time and trouble to prayerfully prepare a short testimony, you'd be surprised how much you can say in that length of time and how effective it can be for the Lord.

I was called on to give my testimony before a great crowd of people. When I was told I had only two or three minutes, I declined the opportunity because I felt I could not do it in such a short length of time. I had given my testimony hundreds of times when I had ten, fifteen, or twenty minutes, but I had never been called on to give such a short testimony. I realized then that I needed to work on this, so that when the opportunity arose for a short talk I could hit upon a few highlights and still cover the main facts for the glory of God. The following outline might be of help:

1. Briefly share what your life was like before you knew Christ as your Saviour.

2. Briefly tell how you came to the realization you were lost and needed Christ in your life. Quote a scripture, such as Romans 6:23.

3. Tell about your conversion experience. Quote another scripture, such as Romans 10:9-10.

4. Tell about the peace and joy you have had since you accepted Christ, and how he changed your life, and will do the same for them.

Work on this! Write it, and rewrite it, until you have it perfected so you can give it in three minutes. You see, we must train to win. If you go out haphazardly, unprepared, you are not going to be a very effective witness. We need tools to work with when we go out to share Christ, and this three-minute testimony is an effective one. Share it with someone at home until you get it down pat. You will even receive a blessing from the Lord while sharing it with your husband or wife. If you have no one to share it with, stand before a mirror. Give it over and over until you get it perfected.

Then when you are at the supermarket and have a chance to share this with someone, say, "Do you have a minute? May I share something with you?"

Then share with them your personal testimony. You will find that very few people will try to argue with you while you are telling them what Christ means to you—

something you have experienced yourself.

When you have shared your testimony, ask the question, "Have you ever experienced this?"

If he says, "Yes, I have," then rejoice with him.

If he says, "No, I have never experienced anything like that," hand him a tract and tell him that in this tract he will find Scripture verses that will show him how he, too, can experience the saving grace of the Lord Jesus Christ in his life. If you have the time, simply ask him, "May I have a word of prayer with you before I go?"

Hold out your hand! Be courteous! As a rule, people will take your hand and let you pray for them. If not, just say, "It's nice to meet you. Just read the tract, and you, too, can find Christ as Saviour."

Our aim should be to win souls for Christ at every given opportunity. A certain man, when asked the nature of his business, replied, "I have a business by which I support myself, but my main business is to win souls for Christ."

At times it is impossible to even give a short testimony. In crowded places, such as street cars, trains, planes, buses, and large gatherings, it is sometimes not possible to witness, but you can usually hand out a tract. Over every tract, we should breathe a prayer in the name of Jesus. He says, "Whatsoever you ask of the Father in my name, He will give it you." Always carry a good amount of tracts. Always be looking for opportunities to give them away. Thousands have been saved because someone was faithful enough to give them one.

There is one more point that could apply to your testimony. If you can write your testimony down in a short interesting manner, take it to a printer and have your own tract printed. This is not very expensive. You can have your name and address and phone number printed right on it. Then when you meet someone who does not have the time right then to listen to you, just tell him, "Here is my testimony. Read it when you have a chance. God bless you!" Something personal is always effective.

Even when you have the time to give your three-minute testimony, you can leave a tract, also. This will give them double food for thought.

"In the morning sow thy seed, and in the evening withhold not thine hand: for thou knowest not whether shall prosper either this or that, or whether they both shall be alike good" (Eccles. 11:6).

Qualifications for Witnessing

CONCERN FOR THE LOST

There are millions of Christians in the world who don't have a burden for lost humanity. They are not concerned if their next-door neighbor dies and goes to hell. This is a tragic thing. If you know the Lord, ask your next-door neighbor if he knows the Lord. We must be concerned! "And he said unto them, Go ye into all the world, and preach the gospel to every creature" (Mark 16:15).

The world is not just Asia or Europe or Africa. The world is your town, your community. It is all around you. Go and witness to those who are your neighbors. God will bless you and help you.

There are so many ways of witnessing, if we would just be alert. Instead of reading the *Ladies Home Journal* in the beauty shop, you can read the Bible. That is a witness.

Never go into a restaurant to eat without saying the blessing. Just say it quietly, but yet loud enough that people can hear you. You can lift up Jesus this way. "Ye are the salt of the earth. Let your light so shine before men that they may see your good works and glorify your Father which is in heaven."

One time a friend of mine and I were coming from Nashville, Tennessee. When we stopped to eat, we were talking about Jesus. The Bible says, "From the heart, the mouth speaketh." If you have Jesus as Number One in your life, you are going to talk about Him. We were sharing about Jesus while we were having lunch, talking about how good He is. When we got ready to pay, the lady said, "It's already been paid."

My friend asked her who paid for it. She said, "Some man came by and pointed to you two sitting at the table, and said, 'I want to pay for their lunch. It is so refreshing to see people who are not ashamed of Jesus.' "

Many times when you are at a restaurant, there are people listening. If you are talking about Jesus, that's a witness.

Then there is what I call ricochet witnessing. You can be coming down an elevator with a friend, and you can be talking about Jesus. You are talking to your friend, but you are sowing seeds in the ears of the hearers.

Sometimes a friend and I will have it made up when we get on an elevator. I'll ask him, "Do you know Jesus."

He'll say, "Oh, yes, I know Him in a real personal way."

I'll say, "Tell me how you came to know the Lord."

Then he'll begin to tell me about his conversion in the elevator full of people. We are not offending anyone. We are talking low, but they cannot keep from hearing the words that are said. He is joyful and smiling while telling how he was saved, and we are sowing seeds—precious seeds.

WE HAVE TO KNOW THE WORD OF GOD

"Study to show thyself approved unto God, a workman that needeth not to be ashamed, rightly dividing the word of truth" (II Tim. 2:15). God wants us to study the Word. Remember, faith cometh by hearing the Word of

God. We need to feed on the Word. We don't need to train for five years before we go witnessing. Christ said He would be with you, so start witnessing now. With a simple knowledge of the plan of salvation, and with this knowledge in our spirits, we can go out and start winning souls. The only help for humanity is knowing the Word of God, because it will transform them.

WE HAVE TO HAVE PERSONAL PURITY AND DEDICATION

"To the end he may stablish your hearts unblameable in holiness before God, even our Father, at the coming of our Lord Jesus Christ with all his saints" (I Thess. 3:13). It is Christ through us who will change the lives of men, and Christ will not dwell in us and work through us unless we stay clean through the blood of Jesus. We must not have any unconfessed sin in our lives.

Paul tells us in Romans 12:1-2, "I beseech you therefore, brethren, by the mercies of God, that ye present your bodies a living sacrifice, holy, acceptable unto God, which is your reasonable service. And be not conformed to this world: but be ye transformed by the renewing of your mind, that ye may prove what is that good, and acceptable, and perfect, will of God." How do we become transformed? My personal experience is that I became a new creature in Jesus Christ when I was saved, but I truly became transformed years later when I began to get into the Word of God and build my faith, and trust in the Scriptures. Look up the promises of God! Believe they are true, and act like they are true! Then you will be transformed. God is continuing to transform me.

Paul said, "I'm not asking you something that is unreasonable." He said, "It is your *reasonable* service that ye present your bodies a living sacrifice."

WE NEED THE WISDOM OF GOD

Many times our wisdom is not enough. We come up

128

against obstacles, and we need to get direction from God. That is why we do not rely on our own abilities. True, we must train. True, we must study. But there are times when we don't know what to do but the Holy Ghost will tell us. "Take no thought how or what ye shall speak: for it shall be given you in that same hour what ye shall speak" (Matt. 10:19).

"If any of you lack wisdom, let him ask of God, that giveth to all men liberally, and upbraideth not; and it shall be given him" (James 1:5). There have been times when I have run up against problems that I couldn't handle, and I would stop and pray, "Lord, reveal to me what to do." The Lord would reveal it to me, and because I had the mind of the Lord on a certain thing, I was successful in leading many a person to Christ that I would not normally have been able to.

When you are witnessing, you are on a mission for the Lord. He will give you wisdom and strength and everything you need to carry out His command. Just trust Him and leave the results with Him!

WE HAVE TO HAVE FAITH

Expect results when you go out. You are going in Jesus Name, and He is going with you. You can stand on His promises. You believed His word when you were saved. You believed His word when you were healed, and you believed His word when He filled you with His Holy Spirit. Believe His word when He tells you that you will become a fisher of men. Believe what He says about abiding in Him and you will bear much fruit. Believe it when He says to go out into all the world, and He'll go with us. Have faith in God!

CONTROL THE CONVERSATION

We have to know when to talk, and how to talk. If our prospect gets off the track and talks about the ball game, or something else, we must get the conversation

back to the Lord, or we'll lose out. There is a time to talk, but there is also a time to listen. This is very important. Pray for a sensitive spirit and for God's guidance in this.
PRAY

Before you go witnessing, lift up the names of the people you are going to witness to. Pray in the Spirit, and pray with your understanding, also. Ask the Holy Spirit to draw the people to Christ. "Therefore, I say unto you, What things soever ye desire, when ye pray, believe that ye receive them, and ye shall have them" (Mark 11:24).
DO NOT BE A QUITTER—STAY ON THE JOB.

Many times people quit before God can train them. It is good to train and read books on soul-winning, but the main way you are going to learn how to reach others for Christ is by doing it.

Several years ago, I was selling vacuum cleaners. My brother-in-law was training me. "Jimmy," he said, "I have tried to train several people, but most of the time they quit before they get trained." That is the way it is with many people who are witnessing. Before they receive on-the-job training and get skilled, they quit.

It is very important to not be a quitter. "And let us not be weary in well doing, for in due season we shall reap, if we faint not" (Gal. 6:9). When you go out in the name of Jesus, witnessing, whether you see people saved or not, you are still piling up rewards for yourself in Heaven. God has a record of every time you do something for Him and in His name. And remember that we have to leave the results with God. It is all up to Him. Perhaps you are just sowing. Do not be weary and faint if someone else seems to be reaping more than you are. Just be faithful!

Many times when I was selling vacuum cleaners, I would go out and work a week and not make one sale. Then I would go out and in one day make four or five sales. You can get mighty discouraged if you don't get

130

results right away. But be instant in season and out of season.

I was in Muncie, Indiana, holding a witnessing seminar. We had a very good week. Forty people were saved in the door-to-door witnessing. I met a lady who wanted to go with me witnessing, named Judy Seip. She had a ministry of putting music to scripture verses and playing and singing them. But she wanted to know how to win souls.

As we were going down the street looking for an address the church had given us, we noticed a group of young people by a store. I stopped and talked to them about Jesus, and three of them gave their hearts to the Lord. PRAISE THE LORD!

Then we went to look for a family that was reportedly lost. We went according to the instructions on the card, but we could not find them. We were about ready to turn back and give up. (This is where it pays off to put forth a little extra effort and not be a quitter.) Judy said to me, "Jimmy, let's go a little further."

We went another half a mile up the road and found the house we were looking for. We prayed and claimed the promises of God before going in, and bound the devil from hindering us in our witness. We first talked to the mother, and she accepted Jesus as her Saviour. Then, in turn, we led her three daughters to the Lord. Praise the Lord! He is so wonderful! If we had given up just a little too soon, there were four people who would not have been saved that day.

After we got in the car to come back to church, Judy said, "Jimmy I can't believe it! We were gone only a little while, and we led seven people to the Lord."

She saw that it is not hard to witness. It is a pleasure. We need to put forth a little extra effort sometimes.

131

The Great Commission

"... *All power is given unto me in heaven and in earth. Go ye therefore, and teach all nations, baptizing them in the name of the Father, and of the Son, and of the Holy Ghost: teaching them to observe all things whatsoever I have commanded you: and lo, I am with you always, even unto the end of the world" (Matt. 28:18-20).*

These were the last words Jesus said to the eleven disciples and that great company of believers, as they gathered together on a mountain top in Galilee. Just as he commissioned every believer.

In Mark 16:15, we read, "And he said unto them, Go ye into all the world, and preach the gospel to every creature." This is a great commission but He has given us power equal to the task. He said that *all* power was given to Him in heaven and in earth, and we have received of this power. He said the power of the Holy Spirit was to come upon us, and we should be witnesses. And that promise was to "as many as the Lord, our God, shall call" (Acts 2:39).

Jesus has commissioned every pastor, every teacher, every evangelist, every deacon, every Sunday school teacher, every Christian on the face of the earth. We should go forth in the power of the Holy Spirit and capture our Jerusalem for Christ. We should go forth and capture our Judea for Christ, our Samaria for Christ, and the uttermost parts of the earth.

The only way that we will do this is by personal evangelism. God has a place for the great crusades, for the great evangelists, and for the people who go to foreign lands and preach the Gospel. But the individual Christians are the main ones who will make up the great army of God who will go forth and conquer the devil and win souls to Christ.

Do you realize that if you were the only Christian in the world today, and if you would win just one soul to the Lord in one year, and then if the two of you would win one soul each the next year, and then if the four of you would win one each the following year, that in thirty-three years all of the four billion people in the world would be saved?

If all of us who call ourselves Christians would win just one soul this year, think of the rejoicing round the throne! Think how this would stir the heart of God!

The Bible tells us that obedience is better than sacrifice. Those men who were gathered upon that mountain went forth to follow the instructions of Christ. In Acts 5:28, we see that they had gone forth in power and filled all Jerusalem with the doctrine of the Lord Jesus Christ. In other words, they had told nearly everyone there about Jesus and how to be saved. They had obeyed the first part of the great commission. They had captured their city for Christ.

Then we see that persecution came upon them so hard that they were forced to leave this city. Saul of Tarsus was persecuting them so much that they fled to other cities and spread the Gospel wherever they went. There they set up churches. The Scripture says, "They went everywhere preaching the Word."

In Acts 8:5-8 we see an "on fire" deacon, "Then Philip went down to the city of Samaria, and preached Christ unto them. And the people with one accord gave heed unto those things which Philip spake, hearing and seeing the miracles which he did. For unclean spirits, crying with loud voice, came out of many that were possessed with them: and many taken with palsies, and that were lame, were healed. And there was great joy in that city." Here we see the fulfilling of another part of the commission.

Acts 19:10 says, "They continued by the space of two years; so that all they which dwelt in Asia heard the word of the Lord Jesus, both Jews and Greeks." The Gospel was spreading at a terrific rate of speed. Those early Christians were on the march. They were a great and mighty army going forward. They had great power. They had the gifts of the Spirit operating. They cast out devils. They healed the sick. The blind saw, and the lame walked.

When they came to Thessalonica, the rulers of that city began to cry, "These that have turned the world upside down have come hither also." We have scriptural evidence here that they were reaching the world. I am a firm believer that the early church did more relatively in the way of spreading the Gospel in twenty years that we have done from that time until now. They won the people without the aid of television, without the aid of radio, without the aid of a printing press, without the aid of many things that we have today. If we would put our eyes upon Jesus and turn our hearts to Him and begin to witness like the early church, He would empower us to be the great army to win the world in these last days.

Go out and start capturing your city for Christ. God has commissioned us to do it. We are under orders to do it. Every pastor of every church should begin now, if he hasn't already, to reach his people for Christ, to reach that city for Christ. He should say, "We, God's people in this place, claim this city, for Christ. We are people that cannot be hid. Our light is going to shine forth that many people can see the light and power of the resurrected Christ."

We are to go forth and sow the seed. We are to go forth and do the watering. It is God who will give the increase. "It is not by might, nor by power, but by my Spirit, saith the Lord of Hosts." We will go forth and do our best, and leave the rest to God.

In cities all across America, God is supernaturally raising up churches that can reach the people for Christ. These churches are supernatural churches, empowered by the Spirit of God. God is getting his people ready for a great ingathering of the harvest. God wants every local church, regardless of denomination, to take a position on witnessing. Many churches that are doing a seemingly great work in some areas are not doing a very good work in claiming their cities for Christ. We need many more churches to get the vision.

I love to pray for people who are sick. I thank God that He has given me a healing ministry. God has the total man, woman, boy, and girl in mind. But the most important ministry is soul-winning. Every church in America should be a light in their city for Christ and should begin a campaign to sin souls. We should determine that everyone in our city be presented with the Gospel so that no one can stand before the judgment seat of God and say, "I never knew about Jesus."

We are not going to take our cities with great programs, great speakers, or great musical programs, as good as these are in their place. These have been tried, and they have failed. It's going to take power from on high. If we will humble ourselves and pray, God said He would hear our prayers and heal our land. We must obey the command of Christ. We must pray and seek God's face. Then we will receive power like Philip received power. We will take cities like Philip went and took a city. Not by might, or physical power, but by the Spirit of the Living God leading us.

135

We must have supernatural power for a supernatural task that lies ahead of us. We must have the fullness of the Holy Ghost, be baptized in the Spirit. We must be dedicated to the cause of Christ and present our bodies a living sacrifice, holy and acceptable unto God, which is our reasonable service.

There is no stronghold of Satan that cannot be overcome by God's power and His might. We see that Samaria was a stronghold of Satan, but when Philip went down in the power of the Spirit and with the gifts of the Spirit in operation, he captured that city for Christ. The trouble with most of us is that we are lazy. Some things come not forth but by prayers and fasting. When a church gets "on fire" for God, they are willing to fast and do without food for days at a time, and even weeks if it takes it, and to pray many times a day. Then God will surely hear our prayers!

We need to return to cottage prayer meetings or home prayer meetings. A church of 500 should have a prayer meeting in someone's home all through the week. They should be divided up in groups so that there would always be someone praying for revival in their city. They should fast the day they are to have their prayer meeting. When we get on our knees, hungry to see souls saved, we will see an awakening of people coming to Christ.

We need a visitation from God. When we are willing to pay the price, whatever that price might be, God will invade America, and not America only, but the whole world. Christians have a golden opportunity today with four thousand million people in the world. The whole world is in trouble. No one knows where to go or where to look. We just need to take the ball and run with it, so that we can capture our cities for Christ. God is able to convict a whole city and bring it to its knees.

In times past, when we had great men like Spurgeon

or Moody, God would just move into a city and convict it, and whole cities would be won to the Lord. I believe we are going to see that also in these last days. God said He would pour out His Spirit on all flesh. We haven't seen anything yet! He is going to pour out His Spirit without measure. People will be so filled with the Spirit that they will go out in such unity and power that whole cities will be won. If anything is going to be done, we will have to do it. God only works through His people. He could have chosen to use angels, but He didn't. He chose to use us. We are God's people. We are to go forth and do the job He sent us to do.

When Isaiah heard the Lord say, "Whom shall I send, and who will go for us," he said, "Lord, here I am, send me." Let us love God who loved us so much, by saying, "Lord, here I am, send me." Make yourself available to God. Surrender your all to Christ and join His mighty Army. Begin to march against the enemy in the Name of the King of kings and the Lord of lords, the Lord Jesus Christ Almighty.

When God calls a person, He also equips him. When a person joins the Army of the U.S.A., they train and equip him. They don't send him out against the enemy before they issue him his weapons of warfare. Neither does God. He will equip us to do battle with the enemy. We are not fighting against persons made of flesh and blood, but against persons without bodies and evildoers of the unseen world. We need every piece of God's armor against those mighty Satanic beings and great evil princes of darkness who rule this world, and against the huge numbers of wicked spirits in the spirit world.

We will need the strong belt of truth and the breastplate of God's approval to resist the enemy whenever he attacks. Wear shoes that are able to speed you on as you preach the Good News of the peace of God. In every battle you will need faith as your shield to stop the fiery arrows aimed at you by Satan. You will need the helmet of salvation and the sword of the Spirit, which is the Word of God. And when it is all over, you will still be standing up—victorious!

Talk to your pastor or some of your Christian friends and see if you can't get a witness and soul-winning program going in your church or group. Go in the power of the Holy Spirit! Go praying!

Pray always! Ask God for anything in line with what the Holy Spirit wishes. Remind Him of your needs, and keep praying for all Christians everywhere.

The question is: Will you be a member of God's great endtime Army? It is my prayer and my hope that you will be.

To contact the Author write:

Jimmy Maynor Ministries
P. O. Box 2428
Cleveland, Tennessee 37311

If you would like more
teaching on witnessing,
you can order a 12 tape
series for $39.95.

Also a 3 tape series on
Spiritual Warfare for
$10.95.

Write to:

Jimmy Maynor Ministries
P. O. Box 2428
Cleveland, Tennessee 37311